To our husbands the golfers, Todd and Michael,
and to our children Jessica, Rodd and Judd,
thank you for your patience, support, and love.

ABOUT THE AUTHORS

KAY DAVIDOFF-ZIPLOW grew up in Miami Beach, Florida. She is a competitive golfer for over 23 years as is her husband Todd, a real estate investor. As a sports writer, she now divides her time between the West Coast and New York, where their daughter Jessica resides.

LESLIE F. ZINBERG grew up in El Paso, Texas and graduated from the University of Texas at Austin. In addition to being an Interior Designer, she is the co-author of two parenting books. Leslie lives in Los Angeles with her husband, Michael, who is a director. They are the proud parents of two sons, Judd and Rodd.

CONTENTS

ACKNOWLEDGEMENTS

The authors would like to thank each one of the contributors of this book for their cooperation, enthusiasm and support. Every one of these professional golfers and their wives provided a depth of passion and were eager to be part of an unusual venture. We deeply appreciate all of their efforts.

Special thanks to…

Tom and Melissa Lehman for their tireless efforts in championing *Life with a Swinger;*

Cyndi Carter and Pam Tewell for their support;

Rodd Zinberg and Charlotte Leon for their original artwork featured in the proposals;

Vicky Waldorf for her assistance with the proposed photo pages;

Arnold Palmer, Jack Nicklaus, Dick Ebersol, Ben Crenshaw, David F. Wright, Ph.D., Don Ohlmeyer, and Mark Frost for their endorsements and confirmation;

Marion Winslow for her amazing technical skills;

Erin, Ryan, Michael, and Tammee at Clock Tower Press for their assistance, encouragement, and attention to detail;

and our heartfelt appreciation to Chuck Gelman for his commitment to our book.

CONTRIBUTORS

Jane Adams

John Adams

Donna Archer

George Archer

Leslie Barron

Karen Beck

Cameron Beckman

Jennifer Beckman

Jay Don Blake

Marci Blake

Kimberly Briggs

Cindy Lee Brown

Cyndi Carter

Jim Carter

Billy Casper

Shirley Casper

Jackie Cochran

Joy Conner

Morgan Couch

Fred Couples

Thais Couples

Julie Crenshaw

Jennifer Ralston-Day

Amy DiMarco

Chris DiMarco

Tracey Durant

Bob Duval

Shari Duval

Danny Edwards

Dee Ann Edwards

Lisa Flesch

Steve Flesch

Allison Frazar

K.C. Freeman

Sharon Funk

Courtney Glasson

Blair Gogel

Matt Gogel

Bob Heintz

Nancy Heintz

Cathy Henninger

Bradley Hughes

Laura Hughes

Suzanne Huston

Martha Jenkins

Tom Jenkins

Bonnie Jones

Karen Knox

CONTRIBUTORS (CONTINUED)

Melissa Lehman

Tom Lehman

Judy Levi

Bruce Lietzke

Rosemarie Lietzke

Jamie Loustalot

Tim Loustalot

Roberta Mast

Tammy Mayfair

Jennifer McCarron

Scott McCarron

Kelly Morse

Barbara Nicklaus

Jack Nicklaus

Sharon Ogrin

Jerry Pate

Soozi Pate

David Peoples

Melissa Peoples

Randolyn Reid

Jan Rinker

Larry Rinker

Kim Roberts

Loren Roberts

Deb Sieckmann

Beth Smith

Chris Smith

Crystol Springer

Mike Springer

Mike Standly

Nicole Standly

Molly Sutherland

Ashley Sutton

Hal Sutton

Pam Tewell

David Toms

Sonya Toms

Bob Tway

Tammy Tway

Duffy Waldorf

Vicky Waldorf

Brian Watts

Debbye Watts

Cathy Wiebe

Mark Wiebe

Diane Zoeller

Fuzzy Zoeller

Joanie Zokol

INTRODUCTION

"Remember golf is 95% guts and only about 5% talent."
—Barbara Nicklaus

Some define golf as a passion, others an addiction. Speak to amateur players about golf and they will tell you the game is their narcotic. Speak to spectators and they will recite data on a professional golfer as if they personally are the statisticians for the Tour. Or walk along the ropes at a Tour event and hear the gallery call the professional Tour player by his first name, even though they have never met. Men, women, golfer, and non-golfer, are simply fascinated with this game and its players. This is a sport that embraces any age and any economic level.

But what do we really know about these athletes as human beings? The wives of the professional golfers are the source of strength, support, and information for their husbands. They are the background music that no one has yet to hear. They are the most valuable club in the bag—the club that no one else has ever seen. These ladies have only been considered celebrities because they are married to the Tour professionals. Little attention has been paid to who they are, what they think and what *their* lives are all about. The public has no idea of their many roles as both mom and dad, psychologist, coach, accountant, business manager, caddy, personal trainer, partner/ companion, and the list goes on. *Life with a Swinger* reveals insightful thoughts on love, life and moments beyond the 18th hole.

FOREWORD

Tom Lehman, 2006 Ryder Cup Captain

Every day of my of life as a professional golfer I hear the commentators, golf teachers, instructors, media and fans describe greatness, whether it be evaluating a drive blasted 300 yards down the fairway, or making a 45-foot putt to capture a major championship. Sometimes, I hear the discussions about the winners and losers, tough breaks that come along with this occupation, or simply a comment on the moment of jubilation that may have occurred for a player. It is true that as professionals, we all strive to do our jobs to the best of our ability. We do so with respect and integrity for the history of the sport, while upholding the values that define the honor of the game.

While I agree in principal that as a competitor, we have perhaps at one time or another deserved the use of this adjective to describe a single event, I believe that most of us do not come by greatness naturally. Rather it is a process like purifying gold. In fact, in my opinion, being a great person is not defined by what you have achieved. Byron Nelson is a great man who also happens to be a great golfer. My father is a great man, yet most people have never heard his name. I believe that being a great person, one that reflects goodness, character, and truth, has everything to do with who you are when nobody is looking and when nobody is cheering. It is a matter of who you are, not what you are perceived to be.

And let me open the door on a little secret that I would like to share. When we speak of greatness, my thoughts quickly turn to the wives of the Tour professionals: individuals who reflect and define greatness. They are the ones whose commitment, loyalty, friendship, devotion, courage, independence, forgiveness, kindness, and unconditional love, gives us an opportunity to pursue this occupation which very often is quite difficult. Yet they stand tall, and they stand outside the ropes—they are the cheerleaders, the trainers, the managers of our life, the nutritionists, the mothers of our children, and the list goes on and on. When I think of greatness, I think of these women who influence us as people so we can go out and do what we do best in life and on the golf course.

The wives of the golfers are not celebrities by nature, and are truly the ones who equally deserve the trophies of our labor. I can personally attest that the power and depth of who I am and who I want to be has, to a very large degree, come from the influence of my wife. I would never call myself a great man, although I hope at the end of my days

I will be one. But if I ever get to that Promised Land, my wife will have had a large hand in getting me there. In the pages that follow, you will be embraced by their heartfelt perspectives on life, their depth of character and overwhelmed by their passion. Keep in mind a simple thought—while you've seen the ads on TV where the PGA has coined the phrase "These Guys are Good," let me tell you, my friend, it's time to take a moment and realize

THESE WIVES ARE GREAT!

Out of Bounds

Beyond the 18th hole, far from the practice sessions on the driving range, there exists another facet of life for the golfer, his wife, and their family.

Duffy and I met on the golf course and were golfing buddies. We had such a good time together and both were aspiring professionals. I was only 15 at the time and he was 19. I wasn't allowed to date, but my parents said he could come to our house. Duffy visited daily until my parents finally gave us the "okay" to date. We dated until I was 21 and then got married exactly six years later from our first "date." With four children, there is very little quiet time in our lives right

now...so our special time is to go to a great restaurant in L.A., with a good wine list. Sometimes we make it to a musical or Broadway-type show when they are in L.A. As a family, Duffy and I are just two big kids in the house. We love to play tag with our kids, or a game of football or catch in the back yard. We like to hike or just pick up the kids from school, have the car packed up with sleds, jackets, and gloves and go to the mountains to play in the snow. We love family time and doing fun things on a last-minute whim!

— *Vicky Waldorf*

I used to dunk Diane's hair in the ink wells in first and second grade. I told her she "was my girl." I told everyone. She would laugh me off and thought I was a geek. She just took some time to come to her senses. I was like a fine wine—I had to age a bit until she came to her senses.

— *Fuzzy Zoeller*

It's funny, but when Mark is home we catch up by doing everyday things. Once we get the kids off to school, it may be a trip to the grocery store—sounds exciting, doesn't it? Really, for Mark it's about joining our normal routine and for me it's about having company when I normally don't. It's the same with the kids. Mark takes over the carpool duties, which are a great place to catch up. It is amazing what you learn while driving the kids around. We try to have family dinners, game nights, and maybe catch an Avalanche game—nothing really special, just normal. The most basic things are what we all miss the most when he is away, so that is what we do to reunite.

> *The most basic things are what we all miss the most when he is away, so that is what we do to reunite.*

— *Cathy Wiebe*

Jim and I grew together and I never quite understood what all this was going to bring us. Now we are on the same page. I grew through him and what he was pursuing in his career. All this golf taught us openness. This is what embodies who we are. I met Jim on vacation when I was 14 years old in Sun Valley, Idaho. Jim was playing in the Junior America's Cup Tournament. He had shorts on. It was the second week of the tournament and it had turned freezing. Jim had not brought clothes for the cold weather. I met this guy Jim, and I said to him, "Why don't you meet me at the skating rink tonight at 9 P.M." He said "okay" with a smile. And, wouldn't you know, there I was waiting for him at the rink, and he never comes, never shows. I never knew his last name, nor did I know where he was from. Then I go to ASU and met Jim again during my second semester. I knew I was in love. I told everyone about him.

— *Cyndi Carter*

Melissa is there 24/7 in our partnership. The experience of the Tour is meeting people across the world and being exposed to the community of our world. Even though golf may be my job, it exposes a huge world out there. As big as it is, it is that small. Our traveling across this country and the world has expanded our foundation and perspective on a bigger picture of our world. We should not be so isolated in only experiencing our back door. The first time that we drove by a township on a tract of land in South Africa and my children saw these shanty towns near garbage dumps and filth, they asked me, "Do people really live there, Daddy?"

I told them, "Yes. There are many people in the world who truly have nothing but a piece of tin protecting them." My daughter Rachael wanted to give these children there her underwear since she saw they had none. Their eyes were wide with disbelief that the children were playing in the dirt streets, and Holly wanted to get some toys and give them to the children. This was an eye-opening experience for my children. And to this day, they still remember this. It is these experiences that help to shape and focus and formulate our children as people who will be givers.

—Tom Lehman

Home is where I really relax. One way I relax is fly-fishing. I love to fly-fish. It's a great passion. But my main passion is being with my family. I totally relax when I'm home. My deal is I take my kids in the morning. I pick them up at 3:30, help with the homework, take them to practice, pick up from practice, and drive the carpool. All that stuff is quite relaxing, and helps Cathy out. I always say to her, "I don't know how you do this when I'm not here because this is at least a two-person job." We've got three kids and they don't go in the same directions at the same times on the same days.

I've had some reporters say, "Is that all your wife does?"

And I say, "You've got to be kidding me. You don't get it. Her job is more important and larger than my job. You can't even compare the two. They're not even close."

— *Mark Wiebe*

Bruce and I always *try* to have a date night. It might not happen every week, but it is important. It is nice to be reminded that you're still the one who fills his life with excitement, laughter, and love. Dinnertime plays an important time in our family. Even if it's take-out, it's a time we set aside almost every night to spend together. It's a time to share our days together and catch up on what's going on in the lives of our children.

— *Rosemarie Lietzke*

I find that Dick's time at home between the tournaments is very busy catching up. His office is in our home so we discuss things throughout the day as it happens or on the phone when he's on the road. Evenings are usually filled with the children's activities. They, of course, are all over him when he is home. There doesn't seem to be too much quiet time.

— *Joanie Zokol*

I met Tammy in college. She had no idea what golf was. She was from a small town in Oklahoma where her father was president of a bank. She was into horses and kind of like a farm girl. I remember when we were dating and she asked what I did, and I said, "Golf." She said, "You can't make a living playing golf, can you?" She had no idea what was going on, but obviously, that changed quickly. When I had asked Tammy's father for her hand in mar-

riage, he said, "Well, tell me this again, you make your living playing golf?" Today he and Tammy are my two biggest fans!

— Bob Tway

Homecoming is very important in our home. We always try to keep the first evening home for just us and our son. Sometimes we turn off all the phones. We always have a special date night, and Danny is good with bringing me flowers…Also, I love when he travels and I pick him up at the airport. For me, it is fun to dress up and have a special night planned. It is exciting to see each other when we have been apart for a while…We have some of our best talks when we go to our country club. Danny plays a few holes and I ride in the cart and at the end of the day when no one is there, we can watch the sun set.

— Dee Ann Edwards

Almost all of the Senior Tour golfers who travel with their spouse or girlfriend operate as a partnership. My husband has a job to do inside the ropes, and I have my job to do outside. It helps us to remember this is a team—except *he* makes bogeys and *we* make birdies!

— *Shari Duval*

Donna played golf as a girl. I found out recently that my wife does not like to lose, and she knows she can't beat me in golf, so she won't play with me. We have a new war game we play and it's called chess and my grandson got me playing. Donna went out and bought a chess book and started reading up on it. Now we have wars over the chessboard and she's a fierce competitor. She takes my queen, and hits, hits, hits. I never knew this about my wife. Her favorite game on television is "Jeopardy," and she'll sit down and get 35 questions right out of 50. That's pretty common for her, and I'll get three or four right, and I'm perfectly happy to say, "I had a good night. I got three questions right." She had an average night and got 35 right…Donna is very competitive and wants to win at anything she does. I only found that out this year. I get a big kick out of it. I lose graciously and when she loses, she storms into the bathroom, slams the door, and doesn't want to talk to me for ten minutes. And I sit there and laugh. We have a lot of fun at this.

— *George Archer*

> *As much as you love your children, it is always heavenly to go off without them. Just the two of you!*

John and I have a couple, or three, trips that we take each year—just us! As much as you love your children, it is always heavenly to go off without them. *Just the two of you!*

— *Suzanne Huston*

There's a routine that helps me to shut down and tune out golf when I come home. I drop my bag in the house and my suitcase doesn't get unpacked until my wife Nancy kicks my butt and makes me! She's a list person and my job when I get home is to help her catch up. My family comes first and my golf second. I usually get sick of golf by the year-end and I tell my friends and family that I don't want to be out on the golf course at that time. I think some guys might play golf because they have nothing else to do. I made a conscious career choice to be a professional athlete rather than having a career in golf.

My family comes first and my golf second. I usually get sick of golf by the year-end...

— Bob Heintz

Changes are so rapid in this game, but you don't think about it. We are still growing up together. Please understand what that means to us as a couple then and now. I know that Jack is coming home to me in the evening and he knows that I will be there for him. That's what I am talking about. Our perspective despite being watched publicly doesn't affect or have an effect upon us. We are just Jack and Barbara. We don't think about it.

— Barbara Nicklaus

It's hard for me to watch my son David out on the golf course. I am so very proud of him. Oftentimes, and more often than not, we are playing on the same day at the same time, and all I can do to keep track is ask the newscasters or someone what the news is. It's even harder to get in a simple discussion—sometimes it's only voice mail. As a child, David loved baseball, but golf became his true passion. As a club professional, I was able to help him.

— Bob Duval

In the beginning, I have to admit to being a bit star struck. It was so exciting to eat lunch next to all these guys I previously had seen only on TV. In Hawaii, our first event on Tour, the daycare was in a tent very near to the course. As I sat in a rocking chair consoling my distraught P.J., I struck up a conversation with another woman doing the same thing with her child. I didn't find out until later that it was Jesper Parnevik's wife. It has been difficult getting to know many of the other wives and mothers—who has the time? The other reason may be that many of the women make friends with those whose husbands joined the Tour at the same time. This is an amazing, challenging life we lead, with many upsides to offset the difficulties. It is also crazy, sometimes frustrating, and tiring. There is not much glitzy hobnobbing. We are here to do a job—to earn a living and entertain some golf fans along the way.

— *Nancy Heintz*

> *"I don't care if there is a PTA meeting or an exercise class or playtimes or a party that a kid has to get to. When your husband needs you, you go no matter what."*

When I was pregnant with Suzanne in 1992, I will never forget when Barbara Nicklaus came up to me and pointed her finger in my face. She told me she was pointing her finger at me because I would always remember the finger even if I forgot the words. She said, "I don't care if there is a PTA meeting or an exercise class or playtimes or a party that a kid has to get to. When your husband needs you, you go no matter what." And I never forgot that. That is the crux of my commitment to my husband and my friend.

— *Nicole Standly*

In 1996, Melissa and I traveled around the country from Tour event to event in a big motor home. We thought this was a way to bring the family together and be together as we visited our country. But that huge motor home kept getting smaller each and every day that we were in it. Homeschooling the kids was way too difficult, and so, at the end of the time traveling around, Melissa and the kids went back to Florida and I took it for the remainder of the Tour stops. After all, the kids didn't want to go to some of the places the events were. We called them "the truck stop tours!"

— *David Peoples*

Quiet moments at our house seem few and far between—but occasionally, they do happen, usually about the time we finally go to sleep. We recently went to Carmel ALONE and NO CLUBS!!!! What a change. That was nice; we really enjoy that! Mike and the kids love getting in the spa together. That is a special time for them, since we rarely use Daddy's spa while he is gone. Usually within a day of his return home, they all are out there having a great time.

— *Crystol Springer*

It sounds funny, but Ben is so busy when he is at home due to his other business ventures and the kids' schedules that when we are on Tour, we relax! It's just us, or, when the kids are with us, it's *pure quality time*—no school, no schedules—Yeah!! Also, when Ben is home, my kids go with him every morning to get coffee and bagels. Then he takes them to school. They love this ritual with him. Our middle child loves to birdwatch with him as well.

— Julie Crenshaw

The Tour used to be a lifestyle, but now it is a job. The Tour players don't mix their job (golf) with their personal life. Today you rarely see golfers mixing this together and it is part of the changes in our society, our changing community of mankind. I remember in 1976 walking to a restaurant with Gene Sarazan and we sat on a park bench talking about everything. He talked about being together and just building a relationship and building that partnership.

— Jerry Pate

Bradley and I will get a babysitter at least once a week, whether we are traveling or not. It's important to maintain "couple time" because it gives you an opportunity to really talk, laugh, whatever, without interruptions from the children. We try to do something as a family at each tournament— maybe go to a park, museum, or zoo. And when we're home, we're *always* busy with preschool, play groups, etc. We try to maintain a routine.

— Laura Hughes

B illy and I are never away from each other for more than a week, and even that is hard. But time spent apart can be a healthy thing. It's really hard to define which are our special moments because so many of them are special. But because we are on the go, go, go, I think that our favorite time

is when Billy, myself, our son Maxwell, and our dogs, Tulsa and Dallas, are in our home all on the couch together.

— Tammy Mayfair

W hen I was first playing golf, it seemed like I was so caught up by it all, and so busy all the time with golf. But when Marci became involved in my life, we consumed ourselves with each other and golf was just something I was working on. Now I have somebody to go sightseeing with, places to enjoy together, and have company, which is something I so look forward to when I get off the golf course. Even when I am most frustrated, I have Marci and our daughter Miranda who travel with me all the time. Off the golf course, my life switches positions and I am more interested in going to McDonald's with her and see her be with other children! In the business of golf, you have to do it all on your own and be pretty self-sufficient. But having my family and my wife Marci there gives me the support system that makes it all worthwhile. I am just a normal person, a quiet guy who likes to come home, put on my Levis and a T-shirt, and get out and drag race.

—Jay Don Blake

To Russ, I am always saying when he comes home, "I have been making all the decisions." So when he is home, I lean on the kids and say, "Go ask your father." That integrates him back in really, really fast.

Now let's face it, if he has been out for four straight weeks and hasn't been doing well and his playing stinks, when he gets home, I always tease him and say, "Russ baby, you don't look so good."

And then he will turn to me and say, "Hey baby, on the contrary, you look really, really, good!" Then we share a quick laugh together.

— *Jackie Cochran*

Laura and I don't get a lot of time just for the two of us. It's good on weeks like the Disney because we used to live there and we have a lot of friends in Orlando. We're organized there because we have babysitters we used to use. But it's difficult with the kids, you have to try and make your own space as well. We try and do that. I think we do a pretty good job of it. That's one of the reasons we moved to Connecticut as well, because we have more family and more babysitters and cousins the kids can play with, and we can still have time for ourselves.

— *Bradley Hughes*

Getting away and having some time just with Amy and myself is probably one of the most difficult things in our life. Since we have had children, we haven't really had too much "Amy and Chris time"—at least that's what I call it. Now that they are a little older, Amy's mother travels with us, so we get some one-on-one time. Hawaii is the best. That becomes full family time. Downtime without clubs is a short ski trip.

— *Chris DiMarco*

My husband Dick and I were high-school sweethearts, and golf has always been in the picture. I remember when I was in high school and he was on the junior college golf team. One day Dick forgot to pick me up from cheerleading practice because he was practicing on the golf course. In an immature huff, I had the foolish audacity to tell him, "It's either golf or me!"

Dick quickly responded with, "I really wish you hadn't said that!"

I stammered out with, "Maybe I better re-think this!"

— *Roberta Mast*

In an immature huff, I had the foolish audacity to tell him, "It's either golf or me!"

Dick quickly responded with, "I really wish you hadn't said that!"

I stammered out with a, "Maybe I better re-think this!"

Jerry and I enjoy going for long walks or spending a day at the beach together. The children love to go snow skiing at Christmas as a family. When the children were small, we would always plan a week at the beach in San Destin. At home, our favorite thing to do is to cook hamburgers and just relax. We like being at home and hanging at home.

— *Soozi Pate*

While at home, Matt and I usually enjoy grilling out on our back patio and having a quiet dinner at home. On the road, I  usually research one fun thing to do in or near that particular city and make it a point to get us there during the week. I feel strongly that our lives cannot be all golf. There has to be a happy medium in life. It is all about balance, for instance, seeing Mother Teresa while in Calcutta, India, or seeing Graceland in Memphis, or even going to the White House in D.C. I think this is very important and we have some wonderful memories.

— *Blair Gogel*

Having a nanny travel with us has been great and so worthwhile. Scott and I are able to go out to dinner alone one night almost every week. Or sometimes we put the kids to bed and eat room service together later so we can talk. We have gotten into the habit of going out together for a gourmet meal the night before a big Sunday round when he's in contention or in the lead. It's fun and filling, and takes his mind off things—plus, we tend to sleep better on a full stomach! Scott and I love to hang out at the pool together with the kids in the late afternoons and early evening. Reading stories together all snuggled in at bedtime is a great ritual, too.

— *Jennifer McCarron*

W e love to talk in bed especially when Chris has been gone for a while. It is hard to stay caught up on the telephone. He is always in a hurry, and I have two children pulling at me when I am on the phone. Dinnertime is a great time to catch up for all four of us. I am a big believer in the family-dinner table time. If Chris is home, I really push for him to be home for dinner. It is a great time to talk about everything.

— Beth Smith

Q uiet times come far and few between in the Ogrin house. David loves to play card games, poker mostly, with the kids. We took the TV out of the living room last year and have not missed it at all. Just turning the thing off gives us such quality time in the evening. We all like to have a special dinner together with candles and name tags. The kids enjoy preparing the setting as Mom fixes their favorite meals.

— Sharon Ogrin

D avid and I usually don't get much quiet time together until Carter goes to bed. When we are home, we will usually go out on a "date" night at least once during the week and that is always nice. When David has been away, the first thing Carter always wants to do is for them to go out in the backyard and play baseball. They also usually go to lunch together at their favorite Mexican restaurant that Carter refers to as "the taco place."

— Sonya Toms

When I come home the first day, I just drop my bags. I saunter into the living room and collapse. Then I move into the bedroom and pass out there for a while. By day two or three, the couch and the bed are the only things that I have seen. I cannot wait to have that time with Beth when we just lay in bed together, not for the sexual aspect of our relationship, but to be close to my companion, to hold her and just talk for hours. Our bed is the place where we communicate, and together we are a couple. I envelope her there and that's what I miss the most when I am out on tour.

When I come home the first day, I just drop my bags. I saunter into the living room and collapse.

— *Chris Smith*

I always try to include Wayne in our children's lives. I schedule their dentists' and doctors' appointments around Wayne's schedule because he wants to take them. Birthdays are always celebrated when Wayne is home. Sometimes they may be a week or two late, but that is important to us. Being both Mom and Dad is a huge responsibility, especially when our children become teenagers. You need that extra voice to back you in your decisions. You pray a lot and hope for the best.

— *Judy Levi*

John and I love good food so we spend our time together cooking. The kids know that when he comes home, we will have something special. His specialty is crawfish pasta—it is so yummy! They have learned to eat a variety of different foods. As a special treat we take them to eat sushi. The kids and John like to fish, either in one of our ponds, or at the lake in the boat. When we lived in Arizona, our vacations would be spent on the lake fishing, skiing and camping with my sister Donna and her husband and children. We'd boat out to an island with everything we needed for three or four days and spend the whole time on that island by ourselves. The only time we saw civilization was when we went to the "ramina" (that's what five-year-old Kimberly would call it) to get gas and ice. On our vacations, Dad left the golf clubs at home.

— Jane Adams

Cam and I met at Texas Lutheran College in Seguin, Texas. My roommate was dating his roommate and before I met Cam, she kept telling me how cute and nice he was and that I *had* to meet him. We were already at school because we started volleyball practice three weeks before classes started, so I hadn't seen him yet. Anyway, there was a party right before the semester started and we were having people over at our apartment first. That was the big setup. There was an immediate

Since Cam doesn't have an 8 to 5 job, he gets to be home during the off-season for almost two months!

attraction! We've been together for ten years now, married almost five. Now that little Hannah is here, our lives have changed. In the past we had a lot of relaxation time, dinners out and going to the movies. Since Cam doesn't have an eight-to-five job, he gets to be home during the off-season for almost two months!

— Jennifer Beckman

Home on the Range

For a Tour wife, being home alone without her husband means she is responsible for everything in their lives: the family, the home, personal management, and for many, their own occupations. After being away for extended periods of time, the Tour player's re-entry can be the biggest challenge of all.

If you as the wife are handling everything and the husband is out there, sometimes he is made to be the stranger. And while I didn't do everything right, I often think that I should have involved Fuzzy in more of the "happenings of the home," the children and our joint responsibilities. Perhaps I made him feel distant in not having a clue of what was really going on with our life. Maybe sometimes I estranged him in the process of doing what was supposed to be good for him. And now, he doesn't have a clue and I can't blame him because I made it that way. So when Fuzzy comes home, he just jumps in and gets to the task. I want his time at home with the children to be quality time together. He loves his children and being part of their lives. When he comes home, he spoils them rotten and then off he goes to the

next tournament and I have to deal with that. Thanks a lot, Fuzzy. But as our children have gotten older, they realize that the disciplinarian—me—is not really the bad one. They now thank me for being grounded. Can you believe that your children get to the point of thanking you for your strength and support? What a wonderful feeling.

— *Diane Zoeller*

You need to have things in the right priority. When Loren's on the road, and I'm at home, I say anytime you get to tell me how to do my job, I get to tell you how to do yours. It's not as intense as it was. I'm competitive but it has mellowed out. These men are working their tails off and they don't need a wife to tell them what to do. I enjoy life. I appreciate the Tour. And as I get older, I appreciate more things. I don't tell Loren every little thing that goes on at home while he's away. What they don't know won't hurt them. I protect Loren.

— *Kim Roberts*

When Loren's on the road, and I'm at home, I say anytime you get to tell me how to do my job, I get to tell you how to do yours.

No way around it, the long absences are really hard. Thursday through Sunday is always a little easier for me because I can follow Danny's play hole by hole on the computer now and sometimes catch him on TV. I'm so thankful for the telephone! We talk at least four times a day. Believe it or not, dinnertime is one of the loneliest times for me when he is gone. You wouldn't think so with feeding five children. It's not quiet, but I hate not seeing him at the other end of the dinner table.

— *Kimberly Briggs*

Being alone is just something that you do! Three weeks after having my third child, I had an interesting day at home—the baby's umbilical cord came off, the middle child lost her tooth and the oldest needed to have a talk about her body changing. Three different people in a mere hour! You handle it and then you communicate it to your spouse. I am fortunate to have a wonderful husband who is supportive, and when he is home he pitches in.

— *Julie Crenshaw*

F amily separation is sometimes harder on the golfer than on the children. David gets very lonely out on tour by himself. We used to travel a lot when the kids were small. We'd drive in a full-sized van from coast to coast. Driving for 14 hours in a day was normal. Our family would play games, watch movies, and sing songs. Just being together as a family was a cherished time. Being both Mom and Dad when David is away is tough. But I live in my hometown and have the benefit of my mom and dad, sister, other relatives, and best friends from school. They are all my strength. I don't know if I could do it all by myself without them.

— *Sharon Ogrin*

H aving Barbara home with the kids and not having her out there with me, that was just part of the deal. I never thought much about it. She always put my career first and then everything else second. As a result, I was free to do what I had to do, which was to play golf, and she did what she had to do. Although we were often separate, we were really working together. I was never away from home for that long a period of time at all way back then, and when I came back home, it was as if I never left at all. That's the way I liked to keep it. It was that way because Barbara engaged that feeling. I spoke to them every day—all the kids. You can't believe all the things that Barbara does, the things that she handles and the way she handles people. I believe that I am a pretty lucky guy to have had all that support from one person for all these years. Who knows what I would have turned out to be if I didn't have her?

I am a pretty lucky guy to have had all that support from one person for all these years. Who knows what I would have turned out to be if I didn't have her?

— *Jack Nicklaus*

When Brian is gone, I'm able to take advantage of that time by myself as I'm very independent. I have girls' nights where my girlfriends and I go to dinner and a movie, or they come over with their kids for play nights. I also catch up with my friends on the telephone and e-mail when he's away. I read and have other hobbies while Brian is gone. I just basically enjoy all my private time by myself and it rejuvenates me. Self-esteem and independence are my strengths that help me.

— *Debbye Watts*

We all call Steve a lot while he is away. And Steve gives instruction, correction, and training right over the phone on many occasions, to back me up and stay involved in the parenting of our children. We pull the children out of school throughout the year so our family can be together on the road. This has helped tremendously. Even if I am disgruntled about Steve's absence, I try to stay positive and uplifting about it to the children. I pray about Steve's return and turn the reins back over to him when he is home. This can be tricky; it takes patience and unconditional love for your spouse!

— *Bonnie Jones*

Everything's here that you've enjoyed. When I came home, Shirley would tell me what to do!

— *Billy Casper*

Duffy's time away from home is the most difficult and since our children are in school full time, we are apart more now than ever before. The kids look to me for everything when he is away. I am the transporter, nurturer, solving their arguments, feeding them, being the nurse if they become sick, and reading the children their bedtime stories. At dinnertime when most husbands get home from their job, I am sitting there with the kids at the dinner table with one empty chair. But we are grateful for our cell phones—it keeps us connected. Having three sons, they naturally rough-house, tumble and play rougher than our daughter Kelli. They usually wear me out when Duffy is away for more than one week at a time. Trying to be both Mom and Dad is extremely difficult, and I'm grateful it is not a full-time situation. When Duffy is home he makes up for the difficult time I sometimes endure during his absences. It's a very big responsibility and exhausting at times.

When Duffy is home he makes up for the difficult time I sometimes endure during his absences.

— *Vicky Waldorf*

Being alone is the most difficult part. The guys travel and you must be both Mom and Dad to your kids and run the household. I mean from being the fix-it man to gardener, to secretary to everything! And after all that, try and find time for yourself! It's a lot to tackle. I think you have to be a soldier. Whatever it takes, you have to be able to pull it off.

— *Cathy Henninger*

To be honest, being the wife of a professional golfer, like being married to a man in any other vocation, has its pros and cons. By far, the most difficult part is the frequent separations and adapting to the coming and going of Dick's schedule and ours. It is rather a negative thought to think that your husband has to leave home in order to earn his living! I have to say how blessed I am to have Dick because he is such a faithful father and husband. Our boys truly are my husband's devoted fan club! They really want to see him do well and are proud of him for many reasons, one of which is his golf. When Dick is at a tournament and playing, it's hard to keep them focused on homeschooling because they want to keep checking his score on the Internet.

Dad is the "fun" coordinator at our house so it's definitely noticeable when he's not here. Our youngest, Jesse, asks for him, especially at bedtime. I tell him Daddy is at a tournament, but he'll be back in a few days. He smiles, puts his two fingers in his mouth, turns over on his tummy and goes to sleep.

— *Roberta Mast*

When George would come home after being away, we would re-territorialize. This was the hardest time for us—the re-entry. I am 5' 4" and he is 6' 6". He felt that he owned this home and it's our kids, and I'm the one that had been there while he wasn't. We'd have to duke it out!

— *Donna Archer*

Definitely, the hardest part is being separated weeks at a time. Having little "at-home" family time is hard. Taking on the responsibilities of both a mother and father ranks close to number one. I keep myself the emotionally strong one and the encourager for the whole family, no matter what is going on. A Tour wife is like being a contestant on a game show—exciting, stressful, with big potential and big disappointment. Helping my boys understand why their dad is gone for so many weeks is not always easy. I have told them that he has a great talent and gift to play golf and that's how he earns a living for our family. I know they sometimes wish he had another kind of job so he could be home more, but they are used to our pattern we have at home.

— Melissa Peoples

Fred and I love to take long walks on the beach with all four dogs and we love to watch the children in their school activities. We do a lot of antiquing, visiting art galleries, and we spend a great deal of time together at the horse shows. Fred really pushed me to get back into horseback riding and to get into the competitive circuit. He is my cheerleader when I am out there showing the horses. In a way, I have the nickname Mrs. Lucky: It's so obvious because I am told that all the time. I know how many women are in love with my husband out there on tour, but I believe there are even more men who are in love with him. That's why I am the lucky one!

— Thais Couples

When I am home with my family in California things are different. It could be just me and my buddies out on a course, just playing for fun, and people will walk by and say, "Hi, Mike. Nice to see you." And I appreciate that.

My son has asked me how so many people know my name and why they say "hi" all the time and why I have to leave home for so long to go to work. I have explained to him as best I could that there aren't any tournaments in Fresno and, since I am a golfer and they watch golf, they know who I am. I tell him it's like his teachers at school. Everybody knows who they are!

Out on tour, I appreciate the audiences and I am flattered when they say "hello" to me. But I don't understand all those autograph seekers. There they are running after me asking me for all kinds of things. "Hey, can I have your hat?" "Can I have your ball?" "Can you sign this?" "Can you sign that?" "Can I have your glove?" And they hand me something to autograph that's already got 75 signatures on it and not too much room for mine. How are they going to read the damn thing anyhow? Doesn't anyone ever say "please" anymore?!

— *Mike Springer*

She is a wonderful mother and friend—she is everything, and without her this would not even be a consideration.

Re-entry for me is easy and I look forward to just jumping right in. My wife, Cyndi, is something. She's a smart woman and cooks great, and I mean great! She is a wonderful mother and friend—she is everything, and without her this would not even be a consideration.

— *Jim Carter*

At the beginning of Chris' golfing career, the money was so tight I didn't feel like there was any way that I could let go of my good job as a mechanical engineer to travel the mini-tours in Florida, where he would go for six to eight weeks at a time. The thought of Florida made my skin crawl. And then, our daughter Abigail came in the middle of the mini-tours so that was a very stressful time. Chris lived in Florida and I lived in Columbus, Ohio. I felt like I was doing everything on my own. I was full-time Mom, Dad, and Mechanical Engineer. It was tough for everyone! There were so many days (maybe months) that I wanted the whole golf thing to go away. Even through it

all, I wouldn't let Chris quit. I knew he wanted to be on the Tour more than anything in the world. We found after about two years that we couldn't be apart as much as we were. We know, even to this day, we do not go more than about three weeks.

— *Beth Smith*

One of the most difficult things to me is when we have to be apart as a family. Carter and I miss David, and he misses us. It's even more difficult when we go to social events at home. David does not get to go with us to the birthday parties, pool parties, and dinner at friends'. Sometimes it's just like being a single parent!

— *Sonya Toms*

Doug was on the road so much that it seemed like he was always missing special events like birthdays, school open houses, music programs, dance recitals, our son Jay's football games and golf tournaments, and even the proms. I carried a lot of guilt over these missed events. Sometimes (it really seemed often) I had to choose the "least important" activity to miss so I could go be with Doug. We tried not to be apart more than two weeks at a time, but that was not always possible. Because he made his living on the road, it was a hard choice to make—come home where he preferred to be, or play, play, play. Ironically, my self-imposed guilt (enough for both of us) was unfounded. The kids say they knew that was just the way it was and both initially took on the same career path as Doug. Interestingly, my dad initially had the hardest time handling Tour life. He used to say, "When is Doug going to get a real job? He needs job security. I had the same job for 35 years." Then, when Doug won his first tournament in 1980, Daddy started saying, "Doug isn't coming home, is he?" He went from thinking Doug was shirking his family responsibilities to thinking that I could handle raising the kids, and Doug was doing a great job. Even to this day, my dad is truly Doug's biggest fan.

— *Pam Tewell*

Tom and I are committed to never go more than two weeks without seeing each other and have stuck to that promise.

The best way for us to handle the long absences is that Tom is not apart from the family for more than two weeks at a time. If he does stay out longer than the two-week period, then I'll plan a trip with just me. And if the kids have a break from school, then we can all be together. But Tom and I are committed to never go more than two weeks without seeing each other and have stuck to that promise. Luckily, I have the help of family and friends if I need it.

— *Melissa Lehman*

It's very difficult to parent toddlers and take care of two babies all by yourself. The situation demands structure, routine and especially discipline. As our daughter Samantha gets older it gets more difficult for her to see her Daddy leave again. I tell her that he's golfing and trying to pay for our food. It's very trying to constantly discipline by yourself, but if you don't, you can bet there will be hell to pay! And it's equally hard for Hal to come home and enforce our "house rules" after being gone— it's utter chaos for everyone concerned if he doesn't teach the kids that he loves them, but they do have to mind him too.

— *Ashley Sutton*

Re-entry for me is the hardest part of all. Everything is going like a ship sailing when I am away and then I come home, and have to jump on. Sometimes it's going a little too fast for me. It is a difficult adjustment for me to start over and over again breaking out of one routine (my job as a golfer), and falling into another responsibility. I wouldn't have it any other way, but sometimes I catch my daughter just rolling her eyes at me in disbelief that I am allowing her to do something that Mom has not allowed when I was away. My comments about the TV programs they watch are not much appreciated. I come home and I know that Kim has done everything to re-organize and get everything straight, and then I walk through the door and I can't help but to want to straighten up.

— *Loren Roberts*

I remember him flying in between rounds to watch the boys in a state football championship.

When Jack turned pro, he made a pact with me that he would never be gone longer than two weeks at a time, because he didn't want his children to all of a sudden grow up and go off to college and say they wished that they had known their father. None of them can say that. Jack is their best friend. He really did accomplish that. He would fly tirelessly across the country for a little league game, and I remember him flying in between rounds to watch the boys in a state football championship. At the time, you never know if your children appreciate it, but I can tell you they talk about all those times. Jack could be exhausted or otherwise, and he was there. We were there as a family, and they realize the sacrifices in life that were made. This is an important theme for golfers—doing the best that you can when you are out at the office on the tee every time, and incorporating the family values together. Let's face it, in this business and job, golf means that the husbands have to be gone and you have to do a lot on your own. Sometimes people will ask me how it feels to be a golf widow, and I don't find that to be the case at all. Jack has made me so much a part of his life, instead of keeping me out. I always wanted to be the wind beneath Jack's wings, as corny as it may sound. I have made the effort to be a part of that portion of his life—that's what I call mutual respect.

— *Barbara Nicklaus*

Before we had children, Tammy and I just packed up and it didn't really matter when we got home or not. Wherever you were was kind of like home, but now it's totally different. My family hardly travels at all anymore. It's funny; there's a routine when I'm gone and there's a routine when I'm home. Tammy takes care of everything when I'm gone, and when I come back it's my turn. I enjoy that. It's me getting up and getting the kids ready for school and she may get to sleep a little bit. She still has her activities going on and I still have mine, but as far as some of those roles, they just kind of reverse. She gets a little bit of a break. This is the life I enjoy. I get the children off to school and then I do whatever I'm going to do. I may go practice, and then when they're out of school, I may go pick them up or be here when they get back. And then they get ready for the afternoon activities, whatever that may be…golf, baseball, gymnastics, and whatever we've got going that day. You just pop into the life.

— *Bob Tway*

When the children were smaller, 5 P.M. to 7 P.M. was THE WORST. Russ was out on tour, and I was there all alone. I am cooking dinner with one hand and doing math problems with another and cleaning up a runny nose with heaven knows what. It's very different when your husband is at home and returns at a regular time each day, and is able to help out. We missed that family time and still do now. I am tired and pulled in so many different directions. Before we had extra money, keeping in touch long distance was a real luxury, but now with free minutes and cell phones, it's a different story. I watched every penny that we could; after all, we never knew what would be.

I remember one day when Russ walked in, I said to the kids, "Oh there's your dad."

And they all asked, "What channel?" Doesn't that sum up a lot?

There is something to be said for separation. He goes away and then comes back; I have to get used to someone sleeping in my bed. I make an effort to keep the kids on track—eat right, sleep right and then boom, Russ comes home and they are up late and eating whatever. I am the disciplinarian and they look to him for fun!

— *Jackie Cochran*

O ver the years I've learned to live with being a Tour wife, but I have never gotten used to it. When Bill and I were dating, he took me to see a movie called *Follow the Sun*, the life story of Ben Hogan and his wife Valerie. He said this is what our life would be like and I told him, "I'll do whatever we need to do to build your career and a life for us." It's hard to be both Mom and Dad. I am the CEO of my household. I'd get into patterns and routines when Bill was out on tour, and then he'd come home and take his rightful hold. He'd want to take the reins. That's tough. If you don't have your feet on the ground, life is superficial. That's why the spiritual life is so important—it lasts longer than the fleeting championships.

— *Shirley Casper*

W e waited seven years to have children so that Bob and I could be together on tour. We were able to see so many places and we did so until our first child was kindergarten age. Our son Kevin traveled everywhere his first five years and Carly was born the year he started school. Bob has had to miss so much of the kids' activities and that is definitely the hardest for all of us. The kids often ask how many more days until Dad's home—so it's like a big countdown. When Kevin was younger, he would cry at bedtime almost every night and would sleep with an 8 x 10 golf picture of Dad wrapped in his arms. And when Carly was four she saw her father on TV and she ran to give the TV set a big hug. I, too, personally count the days.

— *Tammy Tway*

I think it's harder for me than it is on everybody else, because I think you see the machine was working while you were gone. When you come back, you're kind of, well now, I'm back and things can really run smoothly. And you find out everything is running very smoothly. And I think it's hard to jump in.

— *Mark Wiebe*

The most difficult part of being the wife of a professional golfer is the time spent apart. We traveled all the time before the children were born. When our first child, Benjamin, came, I still traveled 90 percent of the time, and when Kimberly came along, I joined John about 50 percent of the time.

Once the kids started school, our time together was cut way back. We still traveled a lot as a family, but poor Daddy had to be gone and would miss many things going on at home that the kids would go through such as the baseball games, gymnastic shows, school plays, you know, all the things that embrace the life of school-aged children. And the best part of being the wife of a professional golfer is the times he gets to be home. He is home for weeks at a time with no nine-to-five job to go to. When he comes home, he's all ours (except for the practicing). The "Honey Do" lists will come out at this point and he would do anything for me. It's like a celebration when he is home.

— Jane Adams

It's overwhelming for me when I come home. I am lost when I get home as to the daily routine. I don't really feel left out, however. But when I am on tour, I get to be the king out there (!) for about half the year. So when I am out there doing my job for half the year, what the king says goes! Then, when I come home I have to just blend in. I have to jump right back into the life of my family instead of sitting back. Now that's hard sometimes.

— Duffy Waldorf

Coming back home is great—things happen. Melissa says, "You just have to jump in, Tom." What I have struggled with is that in some ways I have felt a stranger in my own home. Here I have been away and I come home and time has gone by. Things are running smoothly and then there I am. Life has gone on. It's not that the things at home aren't being done, it's just that life has gone on without me there. So I ask myself constantly, "At what point do you stop chasing your own dreams and start helping your family and children start chasing their dreams?" I have the easy part as a golfer, and it's way easier than what my wife does. Melissa is the plumber, the electrician, the taxi driver, the encourager, and the counselor. She is everything. When I come home, it's like get in here—you are a part of it! Having this job does separate you from your family. Traveling in glitz and glamor is not part of the Tour that is real. It's not a nine-to-five job and the dog isn't bringing your slippers to you after a hard day.

At what point do you stop chasing your own dreams and start helping your family and children start chasing their dreams?

— *Tom Lehman*

Our situation was a little different in the time that has been spent apart. We homeschooled our daughter until the third grade. That way we were traveling with Kenny. We had incredible learning opportunities, and every week we'd have a new adventure to see or do. And when we were at home and Kenny was away, the daily phone calls were a help. Because Michelle traveled at an early age she could remember people and places; they'd have something to talk about. When Kenny came home, he would have special daddy-daughter dates with Michelle and one-on-one time together.

— *Karen Knox*

Re-entry is the very best part of coming home to my wife. We get the kids to sleep as soon as possible and our re-entry is what it's all about, if you know what I mean!

— *Tim Loustalot*

Raising a family with your husband out on the road is the hardest part. Luckily, when my father passed away in Brazil, Frank asked my mother to come and live with us. She agreed and has lived with us for over 26 years now. Not only is she company to me, she has also helped raise our two girls. We have showed them how close a bond should be between mother and daughter. Frank was also very good in that he has phoned home every night and enjoyed talking to the girls and finding out what was going on.

— *Joy Conner*

When the children were younger, they would cry themselves to sleep the night before Dick had to leave. That was difficult for both of us, but I think that Dick really had the hardest time with it. The children are much better now that they are older. I am always sensitive to the first day that Dick leaves the house. I try to keep them busy that day—whether it's a movie, swimming, etc.

— *Joanie Zokol*

Being both Mom and Dad has been my biggest struggle. This is a universal problem for many women. It's no different for any single parent, just on a different level and different circumstances. The fact that Mike isn't here at home is hard on all of us, but it is also very difficult for him. There have been many times he has missed the basic pleasures in our life—the T-ball games, dance recitals, school functions, just to name a few. It's pretty pathetic when you have to listen to a dance recital over a cell phone—but you do what you gotta do. The invention of cellular phones has been a great link in our family. There are days when Cody will be missing his dad and ask to call him. Mike might be hitting balls, but in an instant they are connected. I love that. We stay in touch several times throughout each day and he speaks to both kids every day. I love the way my daughter says "Hi Daddy" when she answers the phone. It melts my heart and I know it does his. We try to focus on how many more days before Daddy will be home and talk about the things that he WON'T miss instead of the things he will.

— *Crystol Springer*

Remember, Mike doesn't have any consistency in his occupation—and we do—so re-entry is a difficult thing to accept. We are evolving as a family and he is out there not part of it, and it isn't his fault. It's an occupational hazard.

— Nicole Standly

It feels so different now than it did 16 years ago! There really have been three stages. The beginning stage in no way prepares you for what lies ahead. There was no way to know how grown-up I was going to have to be once our three children started school! Once again, being naïve was a blessing. Since the kids started school and participate in their own activities, going on the road with Mark is a rare occurrence. My biggest challenge now is filling in for Mark when he can't be here and leaving room for him when he is able to be home. I really want his influence to be felt at all times.

— Cathy Wiebe

> *My biggest challenge now is filling in for Mark when he can't be here and leaving room for him when he is able to be home. I really want his influence to be felt at all times.*

Whenever I come home, the girls are always glad to see me. It's not difficult at all. Samantha's to the point where I'll tell her I'm going to the golf course, and she says, "In Louisiana?" She might be young, but she's smart enough to know that if I'm not going "in Louisiana," that means I'm not coming home. Truly, when I come back in, I don't do things exactly the way Ashley, my wife, would like to see me do them. You know, she's had the children exactly the way she wants them, because she's been doing it on her own.

— Hal Sutton

Re-entry is hard, but I'm getting better at it. But what's hard is when you're on the road you are kind of doing your own thing. Then try to jump right back in to all the things that need to be done, especially when you have come from the West Coast and you're a little jet-lagged. Now you are up at 7 A.M. and you've got lunches to pack, and breakfast to get ready, and there might be something to be signed, or money for a field trip, and all that kind of stuff. You're used to getting your coffee and picking up a newspaper, reading it, and now all of that takes a backseat to doing all the other things. The wives are glad the husband is home so he can help out and do some of the stuff they've been doing all by themselves when you were gone.

— *Larry Rinker*

The pressures of being the wife of a touring golf professional are hard. The travel, the hotels, and the rigid routine when we are on the road are difficult. The courage and strength that I find is my faith, my family and my children. I have a responsibility to my children, especially when Joe is out of town and I really don't have time to think about it all. The children and I stay very busy. Sometimes it's hard being both Mom and Dad. Another thing that helps is both of our families live here in town.

— *Tracey Durant*

I gotta tell you that long distance is not the best way to live—it's not the way to keep up a relationship. You have to really make an effort. I call every day, we catch up and the kids bring me into their life when I'm away. The Tour is not glitz and glamour. Even in the best of accommodations, it isn't the best. Some of those hotel beds leave something to be desired. It's not what the media portrays. Our comforts of home are disjointed. Not everyone is flying private Challengers!

— *Fuzzy Zoeller*

Hey, What About Me?

While the spectator sees the life of the professional golfer as glamorous, in fact, it's a lonely existence, with more obstacles than sand traps.

I am just an everyday person when I am at home. People some-times look at me as a superstar out there on Tour because I play golf better than a few others! I can't wait to get home, sleep in my own bed, have my own pillow, and relax away from all the hoopla of the PGA Tour. I believe that you have to work on one thing at a time, work on another and take it a step at a time.

— *Fred Couples*

The first nine years of Tour life, I cried every time Doug left. I would try to hold back the tears until he would get out of the car at the airport. But, needless to say, that never happened. The tears started flowing shortly after we started the drive to the airport. I think the kids used to tell Doug that they would take good care of me. Then one day, I just re-alized that I hadn't been crying anymore on the way to the air-port. What a great day! It made it a lot easier for Doug to leave knowing that I was in control. During those child-rearing years, it was hard to be both Mom and Dad at times—it was very much like being a single parent.

— *Pam Tewell*

The truth is, Steve helps me to find the courage and strength. He takes a risk every day when he is out on Tour. It also takes perspective to withstand the pressures of this life. I am a great believer that since golf is not number one in my life, I don't personally get lost in the shuffle. Sure, the disappointments in life sting at first, but that creates encouragement. I will always find something uplifting to pass along to our children. There is a strong motivation there when you are on your own in decision-making. God helps me through this.

> *It also takes perspective to withstand the pressures of this life.*

— *Bonnie Jones*

I started playing golf as a young boy in Australia when I was about ten years old. When I was 15, I actually qualified for an event similar to PGA Tour events in the United States. I sort of grew up early in golfing terms, I guess. We didn't have a college system at home that incorporated sports—it was purely academic. I got used to traveling around the world playing golf as an Australian, and I learned all the tricks of the trade. Having this experience starting at 17 makes you grow up a bit quicker. I had to learn how to travel alone, and do it all on my own.

— *Bradley Hughes*

I am a wife, mother, daughter and friend. I take care of all our bills, help with the taxes and handle the majority of our hotel and flight reservations. I guess you could say that I am even a part-time business manager. However, I have my own hobbies and passions, including my own personal and spiritual goals in life. This is who I am.

— *Sonya Toms*

I'm happy where I am, and in ten years, I hope to be on my boat in the waters off the Florida coast, pulling in redfish and trout! After all, isn't playing on the Tour retirement?

— *Bob Duval*

I made a commitment even before I got married that being a husband and a father is a priority. I played for six years before I was married, and then two years when I first got married. I satisfied my ego and my golf goals 100 percent in those first eight years. I was almost 30 when I got married and almost 32 when we had our kids. I was ready to move on to be a father and a husband. I moved golf way back on my priority list. The Tour life is tough anyway. It would be even harder with the kids tugging at my heart. For me, the timing was great. As a matter of fact, golf was so important to me in those early years, I didn't date much at all. I feel fortunate that I play a sport where I can call all the shots!

— *Bruce Lietzke*

You must have a good sense of self to find the courage and strength to be in this business, but you must also have a tremendous love and respect for each other.

— *Jamie Loustalot*

Being a Tour wife is who I am. I feel that it's the same as being anybody's wife, be it a lawyer, marine biologist, salesman or whatever. The commitment I have to Tom's career is that I'll do whatever it takes in order for him to achieve his goals. For us, that has meant many years of playing on different tours throughout the country and throughout the world, all of which I was willing to do to see that Tom could have his best chances at being successful at what he loved to do. Tom and I work together as a team. We include each other in every decision we have together in this life, and I believe that as long as our focus is each other and we continue to have mutual respect for each other together and as individuals, then together we can continue to work for common goals.

— *Melissa Lehman*

Hey, what about ME? I'm his wife! I washed and ironed those clothes he has on. I'm the only one that wished him luck before he left, and I'm the one who whistled and cheered when the putts dropped.

I think that you give up some of your own personal identity when you go into this lifestyle. Some you can hide, some you can never get back. I think everyone out there goes through those periods when you get down and it's hard to get back up. When Mike plays good, it's all about him. I've just stood outside the ropes on the golf course and watched like all the other spectators. Hey, what about ME? I'm his wife! I washed and ironed those clothes he has on. I'm the only one that wished him luck before he left, and I'm the one who whistled and cheered when the putts dropped. Yes, that was ME!! But who is listening? All the other Tour wives have done that same thing week in and week out.

— *Crystol Springer*

Since Fred's career is so much traveling, there is really no place like home. My job is so small compared to what a grand life we have together. As Tour wives, we have a gift, our husbands come home for a week or two at a time, and we get to have them all to ourselves. When Fred has to leave to do his thing, he can go out there on tour and fill his cup, and I can fill my cup while he is gone. When he's home, together we can fill each others' cups. My strength comes from an inner feeling that knowing no matter what happens, it will all work out. We have each other, our children and this amazing wonderful life. I am constantly grateful for it all. It's all in your attitude, and how you perceive things. The support and strength from your family, your children, helps to remember that life is all about give and take—an equal balance of both.

> *As Tour wives, we have a gift, our husbands come home for a week or two at a time, and we get to have them all to ourselves.*

— *Thais Couples*

Loneliness is the filthiest word out there on tour, and most golfers won't talk about it, because quite frankly, it's too depressing to talk about. Plain and simple, if I had to summarize the life of a Tour player, I'd use that word. So there it is—a secret that no one will share with another. I am not referring to the wonderful opportunities of new places and people, or meeting the players that you tee up with, but rather the nature of the job and its lifestyle. I do feel fortunate to be a professional golfer, but its one man's venture and journey all by himself from start to finish.

— *Chris Smith*

The most interesting thing about this sport is that the players are all playing against the course, and you are rated so to speak. Your finish is determined as to how you stack up against the other players, but yet, the competition is really how you played against the course. In any other sport you are playing against another team comprised of people and there are people to back you up or participate with you. In that sense, golf gives you the feeling that all you are going to do is perform a job and go to work each and every time you step on the first tee. As players we are all in different directions, but all trying to do the best at the job that is before us. And it just happens to be that what we do is just how we end up against each other. The uniqueness of what the Tour offers us is that no one individual is responsible for whether I shoot 62 that day or 82. It's all up to us as individuals and that is what separates this job from others. No one is running the bases for you, throwing you a bad pass, or trying to make a second down—it's just you.

— *Duffy Waldorf*

While I have no control over what happens good or bad to Brian on the golf course, I withstand the pressures by always being positive about our life together.

Having the strength from within helps to maintain that strong sense of self-esteem that I find is so important. While I have no control over what happens—good or bad—to Brian on the golf course, I withstand the pressures by always being positive about our life together. My motto is you have to take the good with the bad, and I believe there has to be a storm before there can be a rainbow. Just let anything negative roll off your back because, if you are happy with yourself, your family, your friends, and your life, nothing else matters.

— *Debbye Watts*

I constantly remind myself that we are really blessed to experience this lifestyle on the Tour. It's easy to get lost in a world that is focused on your husband. We try to talk about golf as our business. I am very much involved in the finance end as well as other aspects of the business. Staying involved is key. Remembering who you are and where you came from is also key. My husband knows that I walk behind no one. I'm not a wallflower—I am a side-by-side partner all the way.

— *Jamie Loustalot*

Yeah, I get lonely, but this is the only life I've known since I've been 17 or 18 years old. In college golf you do a lot of the same thing. You're gone a lot. When I played on the mini-tours, it was very lonely. You're not playing for very much money, and have to learn to be patient. You learn to do the best you can. The PGA Tour is a little bit busier, and there's an awful lot going on—people pulling you this way and that way. Everyone's wanting your time. It's a little faster pace of life than you would think, but I definitely get lonely. That's why we have these cell phones, and friends. That way I can keep in touch all the time, and know what's going on at home for sure.

— *David Toms*

I am a firm believer that you have to always remember who you are and where you came from. Matt and I are very grounded people. We were both raised in the Midwest with solid morals and values. But I can say that I never pictured myself as a Tour wife while growing up. I grew up in a very traditional banking family and never dreamt that I would marry a pro athlete! In fact my whole family loves golf, but when I was little I hated this game and refused to play. I guess you can't control when love takes over. My family thought it was very funny when I came home with a golfer. I joke with my friends that I am part wife/part psychologist. I should have majored in Psychology rather than English. You have to make sure not to lose your identity or sense of self while out on the road. It is very tough to dedicate yourself day in and day out to your husband and his career without losing a little of yourself. We have tried many different formulas for what works in our relationship. I have worked full time, part-time, and even caddied. I have found that being together is the most important thing for us. However, in order to be together, I have to sacrifice my career. I find that when I start to feel lost when we are on the road and I need to take a break, I'll go home and regroup.

It is very tough to dedicate yourself day in and day out to your husband and his career without losing a little of yourself.

— *Blair Gogel*

I am fortunate; my husband has included me in everything. Be confident in yourself, you are a huge part of his life. Keep telling him he would be absolutely no one if it wasn't for you—Ha! As women today, we have far more opportunities than women had even ten years ago. Together, more women need to have the courage to come forward to bring different issues to the forefront and continue discussions to improve our lives.

— *Judy Levi*

It was tough out there when I was 41 playing against all the young guys. I decided I needed a break at that time. When I haven't played well I try to analyze what has gone wrong. I have to find the elements that went wrong, think about it, and take the time to reflect about why, and what happened. After that, I am ready to move on. Sometimes I'm not all that respectful to myself. Competing at this level requires me to be driven. You don't find very many professional athletes that don't get very upset with themselves, and it's expected. It's this personal drive that makes you go farther and work harder.

— *Danny Edwards*

Having grown up around golf, I understood from the start that if it were easy there would be no Tour. So I have expected the peaks and valleys. That's not to say I don't get goose bumps when Glen makes an eagle, and I dread when we play bad—but I also remember that golf is just a game. Being very outgoing, I immerse myself in interests and projects such as volunteer work where I can roll up my sleeves

and do the things that it's hard to get others to do. While I am Glen Day's wife to some people, Glen becomes Jennifer Ralston-Day's husband, and I get recognized for who I am.

— *Jennifer Ralston-Day*

I do not think of myself as a celebrity. Yes, it is nice to have fans, but they really do not know me as a person. The idea of hero worship because I am a golfer is not something I am comfortable with. And, maybe if they really knew me, perhaps they wouldn't even like me at all! We are all human—at least I am. We make mistakes and the big picture is that we are not special or different.

— *Tom Lehman*

I believe that I am the most atypical "Tour wife" there is! I am far more like the rest of the world than like a Tour wife. I remember one of the wives of another rookie that got his card at the same Tour school that Billy Ray did, telling me when it was over that I was now a "Tour wife." I had no idea what that meant! So, I have found the strength to be a Tour wife, and always have, by steadfastly maintaining my own identity and life away from the Tour. In Billy Ray's seasons on the Tour, I have traveled full time for only two years! In subsequent years, I have taught school, gotten my master's, and been a stay-at-home mom. I have always been proud of my husband and his accomplishments in golf. But in our situation, it was best for me not to travel full time and keep things in order for Billy Ray here—"keep the home fires burning." So, I withstand the pressures of being married to a professional golfer by considering his profession as just that—a job—and it is not the definition of our existence. He has drawn strength knowing that I am at home keeping things in order for him here.

— *Cindy Lee Brown*

The profile of a Tour wife could have been that of a "Stepford Wife." It sucks you in easily. If you self-actualize, you can put your marriage in jeopardy. You have to be willing to be alone and not be a cause of stress. George and I had no help. Being away from each other is difficult. You can miscommunicate with each other. I wanted to clear the decks for him so he could perform the very best. My daughters call me a '50s woman. Identity was not a concern for me. In the '50s few thought about identity. The sociology of America changed in the '60s. We were more the caretaking generation. Those pressures were terrifying also. We were kind of out because we weren't the self-actualized women. I was always grateful that I was a young mom in the '60s and that I wasn't at Berkeley. Don't know what would have happened if I had been there. I went back to school in the '70s. I had to do something. I received my Administrative Assistant's certificate. George had back surgery at that time and I thought, what if George couldn't walk, let alone play golf? I might have had to support the family!

— *Donna Archer*

So far I've maintained my own identity very easily. My husband Bradley is the one who is in the public eye! I try to do the things that make us happy, and don't worry about what others think. It's important to remember to be yourself and be happy and enjoy each moment. But I do hate the long absences. We try not to go longer than three weeks. It's too hard on the children and, of course, for me there's absolutely no rest. Sometimes I feel as if I'm a single parent. But I knew what I was getting into marrying a professional golfer, so I just make the best of everything!

— *Laura Hughes*

There is always so much doubt as a golfer out there. Do you concentrate on being generous to the family or just remain selfish to your career? I was at Westchester in 2002 and had a great round on opening day. I was going into Friday one shot off the lead and then the rain came all day. I was able to complete three holes in the evening and knew Saturday was going to be a very, very long day. I spent most of my rain delay going about personal business waiting for Nancy and the kids to get into New York. There I am with my family and everyone is tired from traveling and our bedtime didn't happen until well over 1 A.M. When my 7 A.M. tee time rolled around, I played so awful I ended up missing the cut. If only I had done my damn job, everyone would be happy.

This is the constant battle for the golfer...in a split second you can become yesterday's news and nobody cares.

Could I use them as an excuse for my poor performance? Should I be a selfish ass and go on tour for three to four weeks at a time and get submerged? This is the constant battle for the golfer. I mean, one day you could be in the interview room being a hot shot with the media, or screw up. In a split second you can become yesterday's news and nobody cares.

— *Bob Heintz*

It's important to me not to travel full time. I only go about half the time or about 15 tournaments a year. I traveled on the Nike Tour and was Doug's caddie for about one year. My own identity went out the window. We were engaged and realized that if I kept on as caddie, then there would be no wedding! I wasn't cut out to be a full-time Tour wife. I have too many interests and things that I miss when I am out on the road. I am very creative and it is hard to be so while traveling.

— *Leslie Barron*

Living in Denver with the Broncos, Rockies, Nuggets and Avalanche, golf gets little attention. For the most part I enjoy that. I never have to question peoples' motives, and I do appreciate that. I have never, ever wrapped my own identity with Mark's. The wife of a professional golfer is just one of the things I am. I am a friend, an athlete, a sister, a daughter, a volunteer and most importantly, a mother.

I have never been one who needs something big to define myself. I take my job as a mother very seriously. The circumstances we are under make my job so important because our kids need a constant and my job is to give them just that. My job is not to be out looking for glory or accolades elsewhere; it is to be available for the kids right here, right now. Besides, I will have plenty of time to embark on my career as the first woman sumo wrestler later!

— *Cathy Wiebe*

S ince we have five children, I really don't travel with Danny very often, so I don't really feel the public eye upon me. But I do appreciate all the warm gestures, support, etc., from people that are in my weekly activities. Even when I am at the local grocery, it's so nice to walk in and have someone say, "Hey, Danny played well this

week!" Or even, "We'll keep our eyes on him for next week, and hopefully things will be better." Because I am at home, I'm involved in activities not based around golf. Between five kids

and a golfer, you do have to be very conscious at making some time for yourself. It is harder for the wives who travel full time, since your life is mainly golf. We did that at the beginning before all the kids. For me, I need a home. This gives me a place to have consistency. I need that.

— *Kimberly Briggs*

I just wanted to be a normal father and a husband. I love people, and I enjoy them a lot, maybe not so much when I was younger because I had the pressure to make a living. I gave people the wrong impression that I was a grump. The media thought I was a grump, even though I had fun with them out on tour. They thought I was an ice man on the golf course. You see, my idol was Ben Hogan and he was aloof to the gallery. I didn't show people the time I should have. Now it's totally different!

— *Billy Casper*

I think women in every walk of life are either Mrs. So-and-so, or someone's mother, even if you do maintain a career of your own. Sometimes when I was out there on the course, it would bother me when someone walking down the fairway would ask, "Are you John Adams's wife?" Or, "Do you belong to that big guy out there?" It really depended on who they were and how they asked the question (and how John was playing!) as to how I responded. Life on tour can be tough, but it is also unreal. When things are going good, things can be out of proportion, unreal like a fantasy world. In the real world, people don't cater to your every whim. In the real world, people aren't earning the money that Tour players are making now, whether it be endorsement money or earned official money. You have to make sure to keep your feet on the ground and your head on straight because things might not always be that good. John and I are committed to work together to reach our goals, whether it be golf related or not. Enjoy the moment, and your memories, because there is a real world out there and someday you may have to take part in it.

Enjoy the moment, and your memories, because there is a real world out there and someday you may have to take part in it.

—*Jane Adams*

It's difficult leaving my family when I know they won't be going with me. If I am out there playing well, and winning a lot of money, I can justify the situation. This is what I do and I've got to be gone, and this is how I earn my money. But when I'm out on the road missing cuts and spending weekends in California because it's too far to go all the way back home to Florida and then come back the next week to try again, I really miss my family. When this happens, and I'm not playing well, I think—why am I even out here?

— *Larry Rinker*

I am so very proud of what my husband Ben does and the man that he is. Through his work, he has reached many people with his kindness and knowledge of the game. I get involved with charities that I care for, work at my children's school and maintain close friends on tour and at home. I work in Ben's office handling correspondence, servicing contracts, scheduling, etc., I enjoy working and feeling like I'm adding a bit to society. It's important to rely on yourself, not your husband for self satisfaction. What you'll gain from contributing to your family by having a strong, healthy relationship is substantial to anyone's self-worth. It's a matter of priorities.

— *Julie Crenshaw*

In 1995, Billy had two wins—it was an incredible year, but in 1996 he hadn't won a tournament yet and at the time he was far enough on the money list that he wouldn't have a chance to get to the Tour Championship unless he won at Disney. After a really bad day out on the course at Disney, I just went back to our room and was standing outside in a common area like a patio and felt like I had just been run over by a truck. Billy had just missed the cut. Just then Paul Azinger happened to walk by and he turned and asked, "Are you okay, Tammy?" I responded by telling him all about the day that Billy had just had— missing the cut and on and on. After Paul walked away, I went inside and was reflecting on the moment that had just occurred—realizing how very rude I was to be as caught up in my sad moment. I had never taken the time to ask Paul how he was, how his wife Toni was, or even how his day went. I had read the Azinger book and it was his words that opened my eyes as to what the priorities in life really are. Yes, I love who I am, being Billy's wife, and the support system we have together. It is Billy's loving and nurturing that has guided us together into this journey.

— *Tammy Mayfair*

When I got out of college, I played on the Asian Tour after being disqualified at second stage. There were more possibilities to make money over there than the Nike, and let's face it, the options were a little bit limiting to say the least. The experience was truly awesome. I mean here we were traveling from Singapore one day, and then off to Indonesia the next. Our lifestyle was changing from day to day. It wasn't like we were going from the Doral in Miami driving one hour north to Ft. Lauderdale to play in another event. The food changes (and believe me your stomach would let you know), and the currency changes, and the mode of travel caused you to realize that there was a lot more being asked of you then just checking into a Holiday Inn Express and going off in some courtesy car to a golf course where people were waiting for your arrival. From the bugs, rodents, living and traveling conditions, I believe that it all made me stronger emotionally and physically, and also made me realize the sharpness I needed to excel in order to come back to the States and proceed with my golf profession.

— *Matt Gogel*

Well the one thing that I've learned about life on the Tour is that it's kind of like the weather in Texas, if you don't like it, don't worry, it can change in the blink of an eye! So you just go forward. I never felt that the pressure was on me. My role is more about acceptance, support and love. Coming to this understanding did not happen overnight; it took years.

— *Rosemarie Lietzke*

I am able to maintain a very private life, separate from the Tour. I maintain my own sense of self by actively pursuing my interests outside of golf. I enjoy volunteering in my community and spending time with family and friends. I love to read, entertain and play with my two great kids. I have a close group of friends that I see regularly when I am home. I don't feel my life has changed much in that regard since marrying David.

— *Molly Sutherland*

I think a lot of people think that as a "Tour wife," all we do is travel and generally have the easy life. We do have fun, but it's not the easy life all the time. In fact, at times, it is a very abnormal life. Every weekend we pack up to move to the next tournament. Have you ever flown in an airplane with an 18-month-old, much less once a week? Most people don't really think about that because they are taking the average family vacation. Travel days are rough! And we've stayed in plenty of sleazy hotel rooms. There are plenty of times when the baby has been up all night crying and no one gets sleep because we are all under the same roof. I'm trying to do everything I can so my husband can at least try and play the next day. All I can say is that it can be a zoo.

— *Lisa Flesch*

Hey—out there on the golf course, you are there all by yourself. It's very hard and I mean very difficult to put yourself in this sport in the present, because in golf you are always in the past. Unfortunately the past creeps up all the time. In reflecting back on a particular instance or situation out there on the golf course, I often and more often than not reflect and think about some shot that I hit like crap. And there I am left behind in the moment. These unfortunate thoughts creep into your mind, and I tend to compare all the time. If I am playing well, then I evaluate what options are before me, and if I am playing bad, then I begin to question myself and become more tentative, which isn't my nature at all. I am an aggressive player, and if I can't go out there and play aggressively, then I start thinking thoughts about why I am even out there on the golf course. Even Tiger Woods, one of the best players in the world, will tell you that. You don't always go for the birdie, but you get it really close. That's aggressive play and I have to aspire to that level all the time. A golfer needs to know when you call upon yourself, and think about what you need to do instead of what you want to do. Most times it's the best lesson I can learn.

— *Chris DiMarco*

For me, the biggest challenge is the changeability of our schedule, and it's all out of my control. Over the years I have learned to "go with the flow" and it's been difficult. I was the type of person who liked to start planning Thanksgiving and Christmas as soon as Easter was over! I have learned to "let go" of being in control and that helps. But I still get frustrated from time to time. It's been a real adjustment. For Scott and me, we are together as a team—allowing him to live out his childhood dream. It all becomes worthwhile when Scott looks at me and says, "I couldn't do this without you." And he tells me he can hardly wait until I return to my career dream as a writer so that he can retire!

— *Jennifer McCarron*

I have to remember golf is a learning process and it's stages that you go through. The old cliché, "one shot at a time" says it all. You gotta move on and there are plenty of holes. I can get totally jacked up thinking I just drove a perfect ball 300 yards straight down the middle, and when I get there, it's laying in the biggest #@$&*#* divot you have ever seen. As professional golfers, we have our own unique demeanor—we're kind of a lonely bunch. We spend most of our time doing our job all by ourselves. I make sure that I am not alone when I am away for three to four weeks in a row. I'll stay with my caddie. Yeah, I am out on the golf course playing, but after that, I don't want to be by myself. He's someone to talk to off the course and understands when it's business time or sleep time.

— *Mike Springer*

I never thought that it takes any more courage or strength than any other wife to be out on Tour. I'm sure other professions have their own ups and downs as well. For us, we can never let the pressures of golf control our lives. I am Bill's wife and if the public eye comes with it, then that's how it is. It has never caused me any turmoil. I support him and stand by him in any situation. If I am ignored, then so be it. Actually, I am shy, so I like to be in the background.

— *Courtney Glasson*

Since Larry and I got married rather late in life (he was 30 and I was 34), my personal identity was already well established. We live a very normal life, and I have continued to maintain all of my interests and activities that I enjoyed prior to marriage and have even added some new ones. Larry and I are both independent and enjoy our lives apart as well as our life together! It's a great mix for us, and works well. We feel very fortunate and blessed.

— *Jan Rinker*

Being out on Tour when my children were younger was really hard for me. It was really lonely out on the road, but it would have been much harder if I didn't have a family and was all alone. I think when you have a great wife and a good family, you're never alone because they're always in your thoughts. My wife told me when our girls got to seventh and eighth grades that it was her job to see that the kids are raised right. She wanted to be at home with them, not having someone else doing her job at home. Those were the hardest years because when I had to go from January to June, Donna and I could be apart one or two weeks at a time. I'd go home for a week, and then be on the road for one or two weeks, and those were tough times. But, as long as I could see my wife every week or so, I was okay. One week flies by out there. You're busy. You're working at your golf. We'd talk every night on the phone and I'd keep up with what was going on in the family. I'd say those years were hard on my wife too, being home and raising two teenage girls who can give you a tough time without a dad to put the hammer down. We did a good job. Our girls are very successful, both talented in their own fields. They have lovely families and we are very proud of our children.

— *George Archer*

I want to be home with my family more than I want to be out on Tour, so when I do have to go away and play, I want to make it good quality golf and make it worthwhile.

I've come to a point in my life that my kids are at an age where, although I want to be out on Tour, I really want to be home with them more now than I ever have. I want to be home with my family more than I want to be out on Tour, so when I do have to go away and play, I want to make it good, quality golf and make it worthwhile. And when I play badly, it's very discouraging because I feel like I've wasted a week when maybe I should have been home.

— *Mark Wiebe*

I started designing and selling jewelry when we lived in Dallas about the time Tom started on tour. I would pack up my jewelry supplies and take them on the road with me. I would sit in the hotel room for hours and work on my jewelry. It was a nice diversion; it gets your mind off everything to just relax and be creative. I think it's so important to have your own interests so you aren't thinking about golf 24 hours a day. You need a balance in your life. Now that we have children, I keep extremely busy with them. But in the middle of taking care of everyone else, I believe you need to take time out for yourself. Do something fun, see a movie, have lunch with a friend, take a breather, refocus your energies and get refreshed. You'll have a new perspective on things.

— *Deb Sieckmann*

But in the middle of taking care of everyone else, I believe you need to take time out for yourself.

When you play golf, everyone judges you, even yourself. Golf will have no effect on me as a human being and who I am. After all, even CFOs of big companies have careers where they are inspected as well. Even though I am now considered the number-one guy on tour who has played the most Tour events without a single victory (Bobby Watkins held that title until he won on the Senior Tour), I have come to realize that winning isn't the whole deal. I've thoroughly enjoyed playing golf for all these years, and I have done what I have wanted to do. As I get older, I look forward to the transitions in life; the Senior Tour will give Jane and me an opportunity to see all the people on tour we have missed these past years our children have been growing up, and it will give us a special time to be together just the two of us as we travel and do things that we love to do.

> *Golf will have no effect on me as a human being and who I am.*

— *John Adams*

The golfing Tour life is not something that is concrete. I traveled with Jerry 90 percent of the time with the babies. I got a taste of it all. He would go to Monday qualifying for Tour events where there were three to six spots available with a hundred people qualifying. You love your husband; you take your marriage vows and you follow it for better or for worse. I did what I had to do. My husband always has included me as his partner in life. I believe it's important not to focus on the material things in life. It's equally important to be kind and never feel that you are better than someone else.

— *Soozi Pate*

When I am out there on the golf course in competition, I am there to beat the course, not ask myself to do anything that I am not capable of, and I certainly don't look beyond the fact that there are times in which you have no control over conditions. That's what is different about this sport. Not only does it require an athlete to totally rely on his own personal skills, but you are challenged as to the changing conditions—the turf, the weather, the noise, or anything like that. Our court (unlike basketball) is ever-changing from one day in a practice round to two days later in the final day.

— Mike Standly

While I do admit to playing golf, it is not my passion. I am very competitive and for me to enjoy playing, I would need a lot of practice to get good. But when I'm on the golf course and hear the roar of a Harley go by, I think I would really rather be on my bike.

— Dee Ann Edwards

When Mike comes home, he is so good—he'll try to give me time to myself. At first I didn't get much done because I didn't know where to start, but now I go straight to reading and writing in my journal. It's amazing, after those two things, how rejuvenated I can feel, with no money spent, just time to clear away the cobwebs and refocus on priorities. Now, my personal identity is fed a great deal at home. While I may not have a college degree yet, with all the schedules, activities and personal management that I keep up with, I would make a great CEO.

— *Randolyn Reid*

You come home and you're thrown in! Being a dad is something I value more than golf, to be the best father I can be. I never really thought about being a parent until I came home from the 1998 Calloway Tournament and my son was born with weak lungs. Since he was born early, I was trying to be strong for Lisa. She was out of the hospital and our newborn was left in the hospital. I cherish all my time with my family being a good father and husband. As a perfectionist, it's hard sometimes playing a sport that will never be perfected. Hey, this is my occupation but it isn't the most important thing in the world. It's easy to get caught up in all the hoopla, but the public doesn't care that you have children to feed and diaper. My family is what keeps me balanced and grounded.

— *Steve Flesch*

It's easy to get caught up in all the hoopla, but the public doesn't care that you have children to feed and diaper. My family is what keeps me balanced and grounded.

Crowning Moments

For the Tour players and their spouses, it's not all about the Tour victory and a check. The birth of a baby, companionship and marriage, or just keeping one's Tour card is enough to fill the cup.

Without a doubt, the most memorable moment on tour is the year that Ben won the Masters in 1995. He had just buried his teacher Harvey Penick who had taught him golf since he was seven years old. We were dining at the club at Augusta National and the call came in that Harvey had passed away. Ben had seen him just the week before when he received a putting lesson from Harvey. Ben and I went to the funeral on Wednesday and we came back in time for Ben to tee it up on Thursday. Ben played beautiful golf and seemed to have Harvey watching over him. To this day, Ben says that is the most meaningful thing he could ever do. He won the tournament for Harvey and glorified a man so worthy. The 1999 Ryder Cup was a moment that we too will always cherish. Ben was honored to be Captain of such a great team and be part of a moment in sports that made Americans proud. It was a privilege for Ben and me to serve the PGA and the American team: 12 wonderful players and their wives, and to spend two years planning this special week. While it was a most memorable week from many standpoints, ironically it was the last time that we would see Payne Stewart alive, who Ben and I still grieve over.

Ben says that is the most meaningful thing he could ever do. He won the tournament for Harvey and glorified a man so worthy.

— *Julie Crenshaw*

Bob's win at the Emerald Coast in 1999, the same day his son David won at the Players Championship, was a day I will never forget. A little divine intervention, to say the least! As it relates to golf, and only golf, if asked what would be the ultimate, it would be for Bob to win on the same day as David. It was the first and the "ever only" time for that to happen in any sport—and it became a reality to us.

— *Shari Duval*

Winning the Players Championship and beating Tiger stands out in my life. At the time, one of the things that made it such a big deal was that everyone was making it seem like all the players were going to bow out every time he got right there on the leaderboard, and that basically, nobody could handle the pressure. I felt like not only did Hal Sutton need that, but the golf world needed that as well. I kind of felt like I wasn't playing only for myself, but I was playing for a lot of people.

— *Hal Sutton*

When Steve won the U.S. Open at Oakland Hills in Michigan in 1996, this was definitely the standout highlight of his golf career to date. The beginning of that week started out so poorly, and we were certain that it would be a recipe for disaster golf-wise. We even had to break into the home where we were staying because there was no key where it was supposed to be! And, there was a dog in the basement that we didn't know about. We had locked our own keys in the car. There was no air-conditioning, no TV, and the well water smelled like sulfur. The circumstances, however, caused Steve to focus on his game more than ever. Rather than watching TV (if he could have), Steve read an inspiring Ben Hogan book that a friend had given him about winning the U.S. Open at Oakland Hills. The victory of this tournament was so sweet for us, especially after being off the PGA Tour for nearly three years following a motorcycle accident. It opened so many doors for us, and we felt that it was a gift from God.

— *Bonnie Jones*

> *We had to break into the home where we were staying...there was a dog in the basement that we didn't know about... we had locked our own keys in the car.*

The major in 1962 was very special. Jack beat Arnold Palmer in a playoff, in Arnold's backyard. Maybe Jack came along at either the right time or the wrong time, depending on how you look at it. That day Winnie Palmer and I walked together and formed a friendship over the years that was unbelievable. The evolvement of our special relationship started then and is a moment in my life even more special than the outcome of 72 holes and a playoff that my husband went through! Even the Masters in 1986 was a moving experience—although I couldn't get close on the 18th green to actually see the ball in the hole. The next morning I watched it on tape and seeing my husband and son embrace each other is something that brought me to tears. I mean, here is my husband at age 46 just about written off from golf. He's not supposed to win and not on the "favorite" list anymore, and then to have his son by his side. This is on the top of our special moments for both him and me.

— *Barbara Nicklaus*

In the fall of that year, I pretty much decided I would turn my attitude around and I have never lost my card from that moment.

I would say that winning the 1990 Qualifying School in Palm Springs, after having my worst year out on tour, was a turning point in my life. In the fall of that year, I pretty much decided I would turn my attitude around and I have never lost my card from that moment. Since then, I consider myself a pretty steady player. It wasn't that I had a specifically bad attitude, but I had the wrong one to have in golf! I was seeking perfection every moment and it just doesn't work on the golf course or in trying to be a professional at this sport.

— Duffy Waldorf

When I won the Bob Hope in 1998 after my father passed away on Thanksgiving day, and my wife Thais had just completed her breast cancer treatments, I hadn't picked up a club or wanted to even play golf prior to that January. Winning the Hope was a true blessing, and, of course, my win at the Houston Open in 2003 after a long dry spell produced emotions that I hadn't felt for a very long time.

— Fred Couples

I will never forget the time in 1991 when I got paired with Curtis Strange and Hal Sutton. Here were these two big names in golf— really big shots on the Tour, and then here I was teeing it up with them. I remember that because it was a regulator for what I had achieved and what I had accomplished to be there with those guys. As a golfer, that's something I look to. That's the way I know how I am doing at my job. You could say it's like data processors getting a promotion for all their hard work!

— Mike Standly

When Brian made his Masters debut in 1995, he played great on Saturday and was tied with the leader Ben Crenshaw. It was the most exciting day yet of watching golf. It was all about how important that tournament was to Brian and gave him shivers just being there for the first time. I cried every time the ball went in the hole.

People were watching me with huge grins because they were so happy for us. Having the news media all over me at the end of that round was

something I was not prepared for at all. I was so filled with emotion, and all I could do was cry. The media asked me if I wanted to wear the coveted "green jacket," and I thought they were crazy. Now, I think I might like to try that on for a while!

— Cathy Henninger

The biggest accomplishment for me was my first win in 2001, the Southern Farm Bureau Classic. When I won, I didn't know I could win. It was a jump-start on my career. I went from not winning to winning in the last four holes; I made three birdies.

— Cameron Beckman

For Jim, sharpening his skills on the Hogan Tour was just what he needed back in the early '90s. He'd say that he didn't belong, and I'd remind him that yes, you do belong there. For almost three and a half years, we lived out of a car and traveled from tournament to tournament, and those were some of our best times together, discussing things as we went along. I caddied for Jim and had the best time. I learned a lot about what it was like playing golf. A caddie knows everything. As a caddie, I was inside the ropes, and able to listen to his thought process and experience the whole persona of the golfer—what made him make that shot, and what he thinks after he has executed it. But, I was fired as his caddie when we were at the Hogan Tour in Lake City, Florida. I was four months pregnant. Jim walked up to hit his ball on the first tee and I was holding his forty-pound bag. Everything went blurry and I passed out. After all, I was pregnant! When I woke up, Jim bent down and said, "Honey you're fired." I was simply finished at that point, and a guy on the first tee picked up Jim's bag and off they went down the fairway. I actually felt relieved, to say the least. I still to this day ask to carry his bag. It's the most incredible way to bond—every emotion is something we get to share together.

> *As a caddie, I was inside the ropes, and able to listen to his thought process and experience the whole persona of the golfer*

— *Cyndi Carter*

I enjoyed seeing Bradley win the Australian Masters in 1998. It was the second time that he had won the coveted "gold jacket"—I wasn't there for the first win. It was exciting to see him win in his homeland in front of his family and friends. Now, I am ready for him to win in America so that my family and friends can experience that same excitement!

— *Laura Hughes*

Without a doubt, the highlight for my family has been the 1998 British Open. My husband was playing on the Japan PGA Tour full time and he was away from home for weeks and weeks at a time. It was difficult for us, because our son was just a year old and we were apart for four to five weeks at a time, and Brian missed his family. Japan can be a lonely place with no English TV at all. So now, here we are at the British Open and it's the last round on Sunday and Brian is on the 17th hole. He needs a birdie to tie the leader Mark O'Meara, and he does it! Then on the 18th and last hole, Brian has to get up and down from a difficult lie in a bunker to get into a playoff with Mark and he does beautifully. Even though Brian lost in a four-hole playoff that day, I was a little sad yet ecstatic because my husband had just made enough money to move up on the money list for the PGA Tour. Now he was coming home, finally, after six years in Japan.

My husband had just made enough money to move up on the money list for the PGA Tour. Now he was coming home, finally, after six years in Japan.

— *Debbye Watts*

Playing in the Ryder Cup at Brookline is just about as good as it gets. There is something special about being able to share with others, which makes it so special to have a team of players, wives, and girlfriends working together to reach a common goal. The victory at the Ryder Cup was different than my personal victory at the British Open because there I was all by myself. The Ryder Cup is about doing something together as a team, instead of by yourself. Working as a team, that spirit—and for our country—now that was incredible. It was very American style.

— *Tom Lehman*

O ne of the best things about being a part of professional golf is knowing that so much of what we do goes to charity. I was at the opening of Target House in Memphis. It was opened to serve the families at St. Jude Hospital. I was there to represent the Tour Wives Association because we donated the playground. What a wonderful thing to be a part of. Another highlight for us is Doug's first tourna-

ment his first year on tour, the 1997 Bob Hope Classic. His parents came out to Palm Springs to watch and he played really well. On the final round on Sunday, Doug was paired with Fred Couples and Craig Stadler. It was simply surreal. When they introduced them on the first tee I couldn't believe he was already in this situation as a new member of the Tour. It was an exciting day and wonderful memory for us all.

— Leslie Barron

T he Bay Hill Tournament in 1985 was a memorable moment. Fuzzy had just come back on the Tour after six months of recuperation from back surgery. It had been very questionable as to whether he would even return to golf, ever. Almost like a confirmation that he still could proceed in his job, which he truly loved. I will never forget that. For Fuzzy, it proved that he was competitive and would be able to get on after this crushing blow to his career. This could have been the end, but he's a fighter and he never backed off, so to speak. This milestone validated and answered all the questions that we had together. It was a new beginning for us all.

— Diane Zoeller

Getting my PGA Tour card over here was a really big thing. I finally had made it! My experience overseas in Australia, Europe, and Japan, was kind of like an apprenticeship and I did all of the little stepping-stones to get over here. I turned pro when I was 21 so I played around the world for seven years before I made it full time in America. It's harder to get on the Tour than to stay on the Tour. You know, if you're out there on the Tour and the ability comes through, you can be out there hopefully forever and ever. Getting there is a hurdle and an even bigger accomplishment. Growing up in Australia, it's a big thing to actually play here. I knew I was going to make it eventually.

— *Bradley Hughes*

I suppose winning the 1986 Masters was one of the most significant golfing highlights in my career, even though I have had many special moments. I guess that stands out because no one, including me, expected to win. I hadn't played well for five years, and didn't expect much from myself at all. As it stands, I never equate highlights with golf because, for me the most important part of my life has been the kids—watching them grow, and being involved in their lives. Golf has just been a game that I played, and something I may have played fairly well, but it's still a game and I don't think it's any more than that. The game is a game. You play it to the best of your ability, but let me tell you, bringing kids into the world, raising them and being the right role model in life, is much more important than playing this silly game.

— *Jack Nicklaus*

> *The game is a game. You play it to the best of your ability, but bringing kids into the world, raising them and being the right role model in life, is much more important than playing this silly game.*

The year at TPC was one of our most memorable weeks on tour. Hal was leading from day one, and eagerly going head to head against Tiger. He was mentally and physically prepared. I loved watching him play with total confidence in himself as a golfer who was almost 42 years old. However, as exciting and unforgettable as that win was for me, our girls and all our family is what stands out the most. Sara started walking that Friday morning, and that very same evening, our other twin, Sadie, took her first steps as well. It's almost unheard of for twins to begin walking on the exact same day. It was unforgettable.

— Ashley Sutton

I never overextended our lifestyle. We lived under our means. When George and I got married, I was 18 and he was 22. We had no parental support from our families, and had no money. George was from Northern California and the local people didn't believe in him. They didn't rank George very high. We were an island. George had no swing guru and no manager. We could not pay anyone 20 or 25 percent to help us out. George did eventually get a sponsor who did not take a cut. And George paid back the sponsor in the first year. But he missed the Tour exemption by $1.88. Then three weeks into George's second year he won a tournament. He won the 1965 Lucky International in the fog of his hometown San Francisco in front of everyone, and received an exemption for that year.

— Donna Archer

I will never forget the time I was down in Florida and teed up the ball with Greg Norman and Jack Nicklaus. I mean, there I was with the legends of golf! But getting through Q-School in Palm Springs in 1998 where I chipped in on the last hole to get my Tour card back, will without a doubt, stay in my heart as the most memorable event of my life as a professional golfer. I knew when I was coming to the 17th hole of the qualifying that I needed two pars on each of the last remaining holes to be able to play on the PGA. By the time I got to the 18th hole, I was choking my brains out. With water on the right, I pulled a shot way right, and was left with a chip shot that didn't look possible. But I did it—I chipped in. I had an out-of-body experience. It was the most physically and emotionally draining incident I have ever had. When I finished, I got my phone out and called Beth, and neither one of us could speak.

— *Chris Smith*

While there have been so many golfing highlights and wonderful memories from different tournaments, our girls' milestones outweigh them all. Feeling Whitney kick for the first time at the 1994 Bay Hill Invitational, and then her walking at the 1995 Memorial stand out. And then Christina's first kick at the 1995 International, and her very first steps at the 1997 Pebble Beach. These are the moments that we truly cherish.

— *Jennifer Ralston-Day*

Of course, winning is always a highlight and a special time. It is so fulfilling to be rewarded for all your hard work. There are so many highlights for Tim and me, it's difficult to single out just one. But the most memorable mark for us is the conception of our son in Painesville, Ohio, during a Nike event. No, I won't go into the details—but all I will say is that he was a blessing we weren't expecting!

— *Jamie Loustalot*

My husband Bob wasn't officially on Tour, however, he had qualified through the sectionals at Eastlake to play in the 1999 U.S. Open at Pinehurst. What an incredible accomplishment! Our doctor agreed to hold off inducing labor until the morning after Bob's qualifying round in Atlanta. He drove down to Florida to be with me as I delivered our second child and the next week he left to go play in his first big major tournament, the U.S. Open in Pinehurst, North Carolina. My sister came down from New York to see me and her new nephew and together, with children in tow, we got in the car and headed to the tournament. I could only walk about six holes of the tournament

watching Bob. After all, I couldn't miss the first "major" tournament he was in! After sitting in covered areas to nurse my newborn, I headed to the bleachers at the 18th hole to sit and wait for him. I don't mind saying I was a bit hormonal after childbirth, which only exacerbated my emotional condition when I saw him coming up the 18th. Bob was about a million over par and I was a bawling emotional wreck. When golf is so much a part of your life, this was a thrill to be in your first real "major" Tour event. Bob too was teary-eyed and together we were overcome by the whole experience.

— *Nancy Heintz*

I remember when Jerry won the U.S. Open in 1976. We were only 22 years old and when the interviewer came over to ask me questions, I was so very nervous all I could say was, "My Jerry just won the U.S. Open." After all, we were still newlyweds with all this attention.

— Soozi Pate

My first and only win at the Shearson Lehman Tournament in Torrey Pines was in 1991 and it was a very emotional experience. I had been on Tour for four years, and as a golfer you always wonder, dream, and ask yourself, "What will it be like to win?" I was so caught up in the moment, and I really felt like I was having fun while I was playing. In a way, I was starstruck to see myself up on the leaderboard. I had dreamed about that moment all my life and I wanted to enjoy it all. I wanted to live every second I could, and although Marci and I weren't married at that time, my children Jamie and Bridgette were there with other family members and friends. As I was walking down the 18th, I tried to scan the crowds to find them all. I just wanted them to run up and give me a big hug when I got up on the green, even if I three-putted. Sharing a moment like that with the people you love so very much proves that dreams do come true if you hang in there.

Sharing a moment like that with the people you love so very much proves that dreams do come true if you hang in there.

—Jay Don Blake

Having the opportunity to meet the most incredible people and enjoying the lifestyle has been a highlight for Billy and me. There have been so many—it's truly hard to pick just one—but by far the most incredible highlight for us was bringing our son Max into this world.

— Tammy Mayfair

By far a highlight for Matt and me was during the 1996 Indian Open in Calcutta, India when he was on the Asian Tour. Matt and I met Mother Teresa. It was Sunday when Matt had finished his round and I was talking with the American Consulate outside of the clubhouse. I asked if Mother Teresa really lived in Calcutta. He said, "Yes and you can see her if she is in town." It was as simple as that.

I convinced Matt and one other golfer, Kevin Wentworth, to wake up early with me at 4:30 A.M. so that we could arrive at the 5 A.M. service at the Mother House, which is her convent. Our driver parked on a very busy street and walked us into an alleyway where there was a tiny sign that read, "M. Teresa." We pulled a chain to ring a bell at the house and a nun answered the door and escorted us to a back hallway where we were asked to take off our shoes. We then followed her up some concrete stairs to what looked more like a classroom than a chapel. There were no pews—just mats, which the nuns used to kneel on. I asked our driver who came along where Mother Teresa was and he pointed to the back of the room. There she was, sitting on a plastic milk crate, leaning against the wall.

Once the service was over the nuns retired to their chores, and visitors were invited downstairs for banana bread and tea before dividing up other food to feed the poor. While Matt and Kevin went downstairs to get something to eat, I stayed up in the chapel to wait for Mother Teresa. Our taxi driver said that if I waited outside this little room marked "Private," after Mother Teresa finished her breakfast she would come out to talk. Well sure enough, while Matt was downstairs, Mother Teresa came out of the curtain and blessed me. I was the only person waiting for her so we talked for some time. When Matt and Kevin came back upstairs, there I was, chatting with Mother Teresa. Matt quickly threw the camera to Kevin and we got a picture. It was an amazing experience!

— *Blair Gogel*

The year at the Masters when Loren was close to winning was a very special day for us. He was so nervous that last day, and as we drove down Magnolia Lane on our way to the clubhouse, I didn't want him to know how very nervous I was as well. To make the best out of the moment, I turned to him and said, "Loren, this is a piece of cake." But I was dying inside. I could have thrown up!

— *Kim Roberts*

I remember being in Hilton Head, South Carolina. We had two little girls then and we just had been made aware that our taxes hadn't been paid for two years and this was the third. I was naïve as to how all this ran. This was the old story of the professional athlete focusing on his work and leaving important details to someone else. The amount of money plus penalties and interest was exorbitant to say the least. While we had done fairly well, we had bought a house and started to deal with all the payments associ-ated with an investment. Mike was definitely weighed down, mentally and physically. He'd missed cuts, and we figured it would take us the rest of our lives to dig out of this. We thought we'd have to leave the Tour because we couldn't afford the weekly expenses, and we'd lose our home and everything else. Hilton Head was one of our last chances. But with much prayer and hope, Mike came through there—he went on to make the cut. In time, he kept having good finishes and with careful planning, we paid off that debt, kept our card and our home. This was a miracle I will never forget.

— *Randolyn Reid*

Busting into the top 60 golfers on the PGA Tour and marrying my wife Diane are the most memorable marks in my life. I had achieved goals that took strength and courage every day of my life. Diane was the best thing that ever happened to me. Being in the top 60 meant that I no longer had to go to Monday qualifiers for a specific tournament—that was a real pain in my butt after a while. I mean back in the '70s, we were down and dirty out there on tour getting our knuckles dirty and not knowing ever if you could quite make the grade or reach those levels that you wanted to attain as a professional athlete. Those years certainly sharpened my skills as a golfer and as an individual, and it certainly shaped our constitution.

— Fuzzy Zoeller

A special memory for us was definitely hands down Scott's first Tour win. There's nothing like it—I still grin when I think about it. We were all so thrilled and so was everyone who knows us. Both

Scott and I felt like we were King and Queen for a day!— it was so exciting. Also, I would say that being elected as president of the Tour Wives' Association for the year 2000 was a big thrill and accomplishment for me, particularly because it came from my "peers," the other wives on the Tour. Leading this organization, which raises funds for children's charities, was extremely rewarding for me.

— Jennifer McCarron

If I had to sum up my career, being voted into the world Golf Hall of Fame in 1978 and the PGA Hall of Fame in 1982 (which are now one), would have to be a highlight. These acknowledgements encompass an entire career. When that happens, you are ranked right along with all the great players and people in the world who have contributed to the game of golf. It's an awesome experience to wander through the World Golf Village in St. Augustine, Florida, and through the World Golf Hall of Fame, and to be recognized with all those great players. All this would not have been brought about if I didn't have the support from home, because it's an extremely difficult life being a mother and a wife of a touring professional. To have a husband and a wife that have endured for over 40 years is very special. Everything is against a marriage this long, and a couple staying together. Everyone that has survived shows what special people they are.

— *Billy Casper*

I would probably say my first victory in 1985 was my most important moment in golf. After going to a number of Tour schools, three years' worth, to finally get on the Tour and then to win the following year was huge. My dream as a kid was to win on the Tour. When I won, it was a dream come true.

— *Mark Wiebe*

The 1982 U.S. Open was a big moment for me. I had been on tour for a year and hadn't had any real success. I hadn't finished in the top 25 in the first year in any tournament, and here I am tied for the lead at the U.S. Open after 40 holes. I ended up double bogeying on the 14th hole on Sunday to kind of fall out of it. A local reporter from Orlando came up to me and said if you can birdie two of the last four holes you can get into the Masters. I ended up doing just that, and it was good enough to get into the Masters for the first time and get back in the Open. I finished tied for 15th and it was my best finish in any tournament, and it was in a major and in Pebble Beach. That was a huge moment for me, to play that level of golf in a major championship.

— *Larry Rinker*

Going to the 1991 Southern Open at Calloway Gardens in Georgia was so special for several reasons. There, I had my father with me whose Alzheimer's had somewhat progressed, but in his own way he could enjoy watching his son compete. Having him there and winning the tournament holds a place in my heart that I will always cherish. After the victory, my father turned and asked me, "Do you get paid for that?" My victory qualified me to play in the Masters and although my father accompanied me to Augusta, he was unable to comprehend the significance of playing there. Today, even when I am out on the golf course and I hear some change jingling in someone's pocket, I turn to see my father who is no longer here. And more often than not, if I see the bill of a golf hat from behind a tree, I think that my dad is there watching, but keeping out of the way so that I can do my job.

After the victory, my father turned and asked me, "Do you get paid for that?"

— *David Peoples*

I will always remember the Nike Tour event in 1997 where I earned my PGA Tour card. I was 24th going into the final week and, after failing seven times in Tour school, this particular week gave me a sense of great accomplishment. What was more important than the event that day was the ride home with my wife Lisa. We had an eight-hour drive home and we were both on a high after being presented with a Tour card. There was a special silence during the ride home—together we were celebrating in our own way. We stopped in Knoxville to get something to eat, but we could have driven to Alaska. There wasn't a sense of urgency anymore. Winning the tournament was the sheer satisfaction we both enjoyed.

There was a special silence during the ride home— together we were celebrating in our own way.

— *Steve Flesch*

The first time I laid eyes on my wife Amy in her wedding dress, and the birth of my children have been the highlights of my life. Of course, having my family together with me when there's a victory win is something I hold close to my heart.

— *Chris DiMarco*

In 1985, Mark won the Anheuser Busch tournament, his first. We had only been married for about seven months, and we were just getting our feet wet as newlyweds and on the Tour. It was such a thrill and I had no idea what it all meant; neither one of us did. The main thing was, we could now plan a little for our future. Since all we had was a storage space full of wedding gifts and our Honda Accord, we could find a place to call home. That's when we made the decision to move to Denver.

— *Cathy Wiebe*

I started caddying for Chris in Canada and absolutely loved it. We were a team out there and I really felt like I was a part and doing something. We had no children at the time, and it was my job. From there, I went on and was his caddie for three more years, although he played great, but didn't win. Chris and I both loved it! I had to stop when I became pregnant with our first child. In 1997, Chris won the Ozark Open in Springfield, Missouri, on the Nike Tour. Our son Cristian and I were at the tournament along with my mom and my uncle Chuck. My mom watched Cristian so I could follow Chris—all the way to the last hole where he had to make par to avoid a playoff with Robin Freeman, who had made an eagle on the 18th hole in the group in front of Chris. To win, Chris made a six-footer. It was so great. Cristian and I ran out on the green and gave him a big hug and a kiss. We were so proud of him.

We were a team out there and I really felt like I was a part and doing something.

— *Amy DiMarco*

Just Believe

The path to seeking balance, comfort, and peace enables a depth of strength and integrity to persevere. In this journey, the options are endless.

There are a bunch of psychologists out there, but I think that probably the most helpful professionals are the wives of the professional athletes themselves. You have to remember it's your husband's bad day. But it's yours, in a way, because you're in this together. This can mean just simply being a good listener. It's their deal after all, NOT YOURS. You aren't the one hitting the clubs or making the shots. The most you can do is give love, support, and more love. We can do anything we put our minds to. Remember life isn't a marathon, choose what's important to you and your family and focus on it. In life it's having a positive attitude. Enjoy what God has given you. Believe in yourself and have faith that God has chosen a path for you. Embrace life.

— Julie Crenshaw

The wives of the Tour players go through much more than we as players do. They sit on the sidelines helpless, and when it's good, it's good, but when it's bad, boy do they hear about it. And there's nothing that they can do, nothing at all. We screw up and then there they are, not able to do anything to help. I have the deepest sense of respect for my wife Cyndi. On the outside women are soft and cuddly, but on the inside they possess great strength and courage. They are our companions and friends, always there when we fall down and they themselves carry us as Tour players to make our own little team.

— Jim Carter

On the outside women are soft and cuddly, but on the inside they possess great strength and courage. They are our companions and friends, always there when we fall down and they themselves carry us as Tour players to make our own little team.

Patience is a virtue. Always hope for the best. Have faith in God and his great plan for you and your life. Have the courage to get up every morning and be the best mother, wife and friend you can be.

— Allison Frazar

I can only carry one coin in my pocket, a bunch of white tees, a number one and number three golf balls when I'm playing! I have never done anything else. If anything other than that finds its way into my bag, Joey, my caddie, will just toss it away!

— Fred Couples

Your job as a professional golfer goes beyond just waking up and going off to the office. After all, you are alone out there. It is a big responsibility placed upon the wives. So many alone times for her. You are completely out there alone from start to finish. You have to learn to build strength in your thought processes and discipline yourself. This starts at a very young age when you are playing golf. You develop this deep commitment of discipline and learn to deal with issues by yourself. For me, it is my responsibility to introduce and educate my wife Dee Ann to the nuances of the game, this sport, and what it requires from me. To develop a successful marriage, it is an understanding to be with a professional athlete. It requires a lot of strength.

— Danny Edwards

M y faith in God is what gives me the courage and strength to be the wife of a golfer and to withstand the pressures of this lifestyle. I think you have to live out each day with the best you have to offer of yourself. Surround yourself with people who can encourage and support you to be your best each day. Focus on others and be willing to give of yourself to help and encourage. Last, but not least, give yourself a break from your high expectations when you don't hit the mark!

— *Melissa Peoples*

Y ou know, when you talk about the wives, I really don't know how they do it being married to a professional golfer. My wife Melissa has always gone with the flow. When I was at my lowest and there wasn't much there for me to offer her and I was dragging her in the mess, Melissa was always strong and supportive. Even when I was doing the business of us, I relied on her as well, and I don't think that was fair. But I had no clue about the books, or keeping things orderly in our life. And then there she was, raising our children, minding all our home responsibilities and keeping us on track during our early years on Tour, which were some very difficult times. For Melissa, the trailer park wasn't looking so good. So in those times, my wife was the supportive one to see that I would play golf again, and her enthusiasm made me realize that no matter what, I could go out and do my job. I often look back and wonder how many others would be that supportive to see their man return again to a difficult situation, one that brought severe changes and stormy times to our lives.

> *My wife was the supportive one to see that I would play golf again, and her enthusiasm made me realize that no matter what, I could go out and do my job.*

— *Tom Lehman*

Back in the late '80s I was at Wood Ranch Country Club and saw these Hawaiian-printed hats. Duffy didn't have a hat contract at the time. The hats made me think of Duffy and how he likes to have fun so I bought him this pink one with Hawaiian girls on it and a blue one. He loved them and decided to wear them on tour. The first week he wore them, he had a good tournament and became known for wearing the floral prints. We've always loved Hawaii and he's always loved Hawaiian shirts, so it was a way to express what he likes. And in the early '90s, Duffy had these colored pens, so we thought we would put some designs on his golf balls. He played with them and had a good golf tournament. Every competitive round he has played since then has been with a colored golf ball. In preparing for his tournaments, every night when I'm on the road he places two sleeves of golf balls and a bag of marking pens on a table and this is a big hint that he needs them for the next day. Sometimes I'll get the kids together when we get back home from dinner and have a coloring party. With four kids, we can usually get on a roll and do a dozen in one sitting, 24 golf balls a week (six per round). He doesn't play with marked golf balls in the pro-ams, which has kept it a special thing for only tournament rounds. Floral hats and colored balls are his two things he won't play without.

Every night when I'm on the road he places two sleeves of golf balls and a bag of marking pens on a table and this is a big hint that he needs them for the next day...Floral hats and colored balls are his two things he won't play without.

— *Vicky Waldorf*

I used to have a ritual—I would cross my fingers and never, ever look at the ball. Now I just enjoy the time being there on the golf course and whatever happens is meant to be. I always try to have a smile on my face when Danny looks at me.

— Dee Ann Edwards

The most difficult part is watching your husband play, and wanting him to do the best he can. Prayer gives you hope. Stick by your partner's side—be a listener; even if you don't give advice, give comfort.

— Soozi Pate

I am always saying my prayers. I believe in God's strength to get us through the days of anxiousness and to help us accept and give thanks for the days of joy as well. Barbara Nicklaus is a great inspiration to me. I admire her more than any woman I've met on the Tour. She is always so personable, kind, and sincere. We can all learn from and become a better person by just knowing her.

— Sharon Funk

The Serenity Prayer helps me to gain perspective on what I should be as a person. I live by this. It helps me to be more open and accepting as a human being. "God grant me the strength to accept the things that I cannot change, the courage to change the things that I can, and the wisdom to know the difference."

— *Diane Zoeller*

I won't mark my ball on the green with a nickel. I like nickels fine, but it's just one of those things. I never start a round of golf with a number two ball, not that I don't like number two. I lick my finger before I put on my glove so it holds better. I don't think my wife Sonya has any superstitions!

— *David Toms*

My thoughts are to embrace those feelings of fear during the hard times in life because they will only make you stronger.

If you are a strong woman who believes in yourself, then you can accomplish anything. Women are capable of great strengths, which is why God made us mothers.

— *Debbye Watts*

My mom had said when she was first diagnosed with cancer that God won't give us more than we can handle. In talking with my sister, she said she feels that God will give you more than you can handle. However, during those times, that is when he is carrying you and giving you the strength to get through those difficult times. My thoughts are to embrace those feelings of fear during the hard times in life because they will only make you stronger.

— *Blair Gogel*

When I was born, my mother, who was eighteen at the time, was told by all the little old ladies in my hometown, that I was going to have a special sense. I was born with a membrane over my face or what they called a "veil," and they were certain it had meaning like I would be able to feel and see things that others didn't. I do have these deep intuitive feelings from my heart that direct how I approach all the bumps and grinds we face. After all, there was a time when I didn't know from one day to another if Chris would make a dime out there playing golf, and I have relied on my instincts to manage us. We could be faced with credit card and other debts, or situations that are less than desirable, and I would still find a way to be positive about everything. So when things go sour, and Chris panics or gets angry, or depressed, even when he lost his Tour card, I am the "believer" in the family. I am the optimist. My personal spirituality is what fuels me to keep going and know that things will happen for the better and the outcome will be all right. When Chris oftentimes would comment and ask me why I wasn't as fired up as he—I always would say to him it was because we weren't losing our home,

Sometimes you have to take steps backwards to go forward. Sure, I've been disappointed for him, because his profession is so very hard, but I remind him that we are truly blessed with what we have had together from day one.

and our children are happy and healthy. Sometimes you have to take steps backwards to go forward. Sure, I've been disappointed for him, because his profession is so very hard, but I remind him that we are truly blessed with what we have had together from day one. Maybe women are more in tune with the tests in life that we face each day; I know things will be okay in our lives.

— *Beth Smith*

I would like to tell all the women out there to never forget how important they are. If it weren't for us, I don't know if a lot of men could survive! I feel as a mother, I have the most important and demanding job there is. We are really the ones that hold everything together. Women need to believe in themselves and believe in God.

— *Lisa Flesch*

Remember what the most important things in life are. Always keep your priorities in order—"God, family, golf." That is what has worked for us.

— *Rosemarie Lietzke*

I used to think what I did or didn't do during a round mattered. Now I don't, but I still can't help

The only saving grace may be that in golf, it may be just an adjustment of inches before you begin playing well again.

doing it. I would pick up a stick on a hole and if Bob birdied the hole, I'd think this is a lucky stick...toss it away if he bogeys and find another. I know it sounds stupid, but a round of golf takes a long time. Golf is a tough sport. Play bad, no check. Play bad long enough, no job. The only saving grace may be that in golf, it may be just an adjustment of inches before you begin playing well again.

— *Tammy Tway*

It is great to be a Tour wife. I have never been any other "type" of wife because David has been on tour since we were married. So, really, I don't know any other way. I guess you might say ignorance is bliss! As far as what it takes to withstand the pressures, and find courage and strength, the answer for me is prayer. The Lord gives me the strength that I need to be a good wife, mother and friend.

— *Sonya Toms*

The key to a successful relationship in a marriage is to be a giver in the partnership. Two takers in a relationship won't work, so you seek a balance. That's what Soozi and I do. I think that my wife is the giver, and I have been the taker, because I put golf first in our lives and the "us" second so I could attempt to achieve my expectations in my job. Then about ten years ago, the light bulb went off, and I started to put my faith first, and have now made it a point in my life to be a giver. I still to this day have high expectations in everything I do. I am positive that if I am not happy with my life, then nothing is going to balance out. The strength of our marriage is that we have prioritized what's important. Believe me, I have my faults, but I have to recognize where they are. Someone once asked me if I would rather be right, or if I'd rather be married. I choose to be married! I want to spend the rest of my life enjoying my wife. She completes me.

— *Jerry Pate*

The most difficult part for me at this time of my life is wanting to be on Tour with Mike and yet, wanting to be with the children. I remember when we only had two children and I was going to Morocco with Mike for a tournament. It wasn't going to be possible to take the children, and Mike and I needed some alone time anyway. Nevertheless, leaving them is so very hard. The night before the trip I put the girls to bed, said their prayers and read them stories, and they fell asleep. I sat between their twin beds and just started to cry. I prayed that they would be protected while we were away, and that Mike and I would come home safely. I just sat there in the quiet, and my oldest woke up.

She could tell I was crying and she asked me, "Mommy you're sad because you don't want to leave us tomorrow, do you?"

I said, "No. It's the hardest thing I have to do. I want to be all together, no one missing."

She said, "You go with Daddy, he needs you too. We'll be okay with Grandma and you'll be an even better mommy when you come home."

It was as if I'd received my answer. Out of the mouths of babes come so many great, beautiful yet simple words of wisdom and peace. I gave her a big hug and said, "Thank you, I needed that." Then I kissed her and my older daughter good night. I went in to finish packing and knew I was in the Lord's hands.

— *Randolyn Reid*

You must believe in yourself and believe that whatever situation you are in, you are there for a reason, maybe to teach you patience, maybe to give you strength. My faith in God allows me to trust him in all situations, and to know that everything will work out for the best.

— *Jan Rinker*

Find a little way every week to make a difference in someone's life.

There is no need to feel unproductive

just because you're "only" a Tour wife or traveling around on tour. Visit a hospital or nursing home in each city. Look for opportunities to touch a life.

— *Karen Knox*

My routine only pertains to work. I'm not so particular in life. Kind of cruising. I don't have to have my ducks in a row. However, when I go to the golf course, I try to do the same thing every time. I try to do the same kind of stuff to prepare to play every day. I'll get up in the morning about three hours before I play, have breakfast, do the crossword puzzle. I try to get relaxed. I try to pay attention to what I am exactly doing that minute. If I am showering and washing my hair, I'm really trying to get conscious of what I'm doing. I'm trying to get focused on what my body is doing, what I'm trying to do. Then when I get to the course, I'm relaxed and try to focus. When I get to the putting green, I get three balls in my hand. I'm conscious of throwing them on the green, and I don't start playing till I start to get some awareness. I play a number one ball on the first day, number two on the second day, number three on the third, and number four on day four. That's kind of superstition for me. I play the right number ball for the day.

— *Cameron Beckman*

Being the wife of a Tour pro affords ample opportunity to test both faith and patience. Above all else, I feel that faith in God is an absolute must to be successful in any profession. Without my faith, I honestly do not know how I would have handled the stresses of being married to a professional athlete. Billy Ray has had such an up and down career but I have never really panicked over the rough times. He has always managed to make a great living for our family no matter the circumstance. When one avenue has closed for him, such as having the wrist injury, he found he had great talent in the area of corporate golf. Doing some television work is another means to be in the golf business. Above all, we realize that with prayer and faith in God, we will always be successful. We are truly blessed!

> *Without my faith, I honestly do not know how I would have handled the stresses of being married to a professional athlete.*

Patience was an attribute that took a little more effort for me to learn than having faith did. We were both so young when Billy Ray got his Tour card. He had such a successful amateur career that we expected great things pretty quickly. When things progressed slowly, it was difficult to wait it out until his game developed into being quite competitive with the other players on the Tour. After his injury, we learned a great deal of patience because rehab is a long, hard road after you have had a great deal of success. But as with all things, everything has fallen into place, maybe not as we would have planned it, but for the best. Being a single parent for much of the year has also taught me a great deal of patience in dealing with children. It took a couple of years to adjust to the awesome responsibility of raising a child, but now I truly love what I do.

— *Cindy Lee Brown*

I feel every day I am in fact still learning about patience, hope, faith, and courage. And I love the road we are on. I think life would not be complete without my patience being tested, hoping for something, and having the courage to go on and keeping the faith that we will get there. Look at life's challenges as a positive, and know that all the little things you do make all the difference.

I used to be extremely superstitious as to my position on the golf course—wearing sunglasses, not wearing them, carrying them in the right hand or the left hand, or carrying an umbrella or not carrying one. One day I was walking with Dr. Bob Rotella and he jokingly kidded me about one of my superstitions, and said to me, "Tammy, you could only wish you had that much power." We both laughed. I still catch myself sometimes with a ritual and then I remember what Dr. Bob said and I just laugh at myself.

— *Tammy Mayfair*

Several years ago, my 38-year-old friend lost her husband with five children. She was clueless about everything—insurance, investments, and her current financial situation. I learned very quickly how ignorant we women are, because we are too busy and don't think we need to know and that someone else knows for us. WRONG! Ask a lot of questions, get your wills in order, trust accounts, college accounts and pay yourself first for your future. Protect your family for when their game and their endorsements aren't there. Store away those nuts for the lean years; they creep up when you least expect it.

— *Karen Beck*

The foundation and support that Beth gives me helps me not to be bad to myself. I believe that as I have gotten older and matured, I have less of a temper and things don't bother me as much now. If I hadn't had Beth in my life or her belief in me, I could not have gone on in this profession. Beth has been more supportive of me than I could ever be to a spouse and she has helped me to grow up as a golfer and as a person.

> *If I hadn't had Beth in my life or her belief in me, I could not have gone on in this profession. Beth has been more supportive of me than I could ever be to a spouse and she has helped me to grow up as a golfer and as a person.*

I need to carry around two quarters in my pocket at all times on the golf course. One is a 1929 Standing Liberty and the other is a 1909. The 29 is what I want to shoot for nine holes, and the nine represents only nine putts. I also carry around in my front right pocket two military coins that have special meaning to me personally. Larry Shaw, a Pilot on a CI35 refueling tanker gave me one. It represents friendship and a feeling when I am out on the road on Tour of how very close home is, although I might be so far away. The other military coin was given to me by Buck Kernan, a retired four-star general from the Joint Forces. I had the pleasure of his company as my partner in Pebble Beach, and I believe that the presence of his coin in my pocket encourages leadership and charisma that I hope will rub off on me. As for my little golf rituals, there are a few. I never, ever eat during a round, but maybe I should! I also would never switch balls after a birdie. But I do switch balls immediately after a bogey. And I always mark my balls with the number 15. This represents the number from my high school football jersey in Rochester, Indiana.

— *Chris Smith*

I think it's important just to make the best of whatever the situation is. It takes a strong person to withstand the pressures of this lifestyle. Some days are good and some are bad. You just hope there are more of the good days than bad. You have to believe in your husband, his ability, and his talent to play golf and succeed. So, you just take it one day at a time.

— *Amy DiMarco*

Recently I have sworn off following Mark's progress during tournaments on the Internet. It's just too frustrating to see a score pop up and I have no idea how it happened. However, it's funny to watch our kids. When they follow Mark, they take a lot of credit for how he does. If their hats are on backwards and he makes birdies, then that must be the reason! They are convinced that where they stand, or how they wear their clothing or if their fingers are crossed or not, all have a big effect on the outcome!

— *Cathy Wiebe*

It's funny to watch our kids. When they follow Mark, they take a lot of credit for how he does...They are convinced that where they stand, or how they wear their clothing or if their fingers are crossed or not, all have a big effect on the outcome!

Life is short! Every day is a new opportunity to be your best. My mom will pray with me, cry with me, tell me to "shape up," and help me gain perspective in different situations and circumstances. She has been my inspiration—a real survivor. She rises above. My father committed suicide in 1998, and she has been strong, gracious and her faith in God is solid as a rock. I feel if she can be all those things, I can too.

— *Bonnie Jones*

I don't have many superstitions and I can't think of any rituals. I always make sure not to think ahead too much. When Doug was in contention to win in Rye, New York, I was hoping that he would think about one shot at a time and to breathe! As I followed him that particular day, I pretended to be Doug as he played golf, trying to stay calm and hoping by osmosis or something that he would do the same. If I am at home during a tournament, I don't check the computer until he is at least through hole number four. I don't know why, but I don't want to get too excited or too disappointed right off the bat. Strange?

— *Leslie Barron*

For us, like many, we have traveled a rough road to Tour life. We still have not successfully maintained it. Chris and I met in college. He played golf and was always on the road. So for me and our relationship, we have never known any other way. Before Chris got his PGA Tour card in 1999, I taught fourth grade. I would travel the Nike Tour and caddie during the summers, but months apart during the school year were difficult. Now being able to travel full time is an opportunity we are grateful for. We just take things one day at a time, find the positive in every situation (or try to), and believe.

— *Morgan Couch*

I make my clothes match. And, I used to only use number eight balls. But then I had a bad tournament later on, and I got rid of that superstition. There's too much else to worry about.

— *Bradley Hughes*

Jamie is to be credited with a strong sense of self-confidence. She has never looked to a man for her identification. She was raised with sisters and a single mom. Jamie gave up a position in the advertising business to raise our family and help support the business that I chose. What's important for Jamie and myself is that we have a shared respect for each of us individually and together as a team. We are partners as we pass through this life together. We love each other, and all the money and golf-related things can just go out the window.

— *Tim Loustalot*

We are partners as we pass through this life together. We love each other, and all the money and golf-related things can just go out the window.

I've always had a routine. I'd play number one and number three balls the first day of a round and number two and number four balls the second day. It's like brushing my teeth. Now the numbers on balls have changed with the company I use. I may use one number on the front nine, and another number on the back nine, odd numbers one day, and even the next day.

— *Billy Casper*

We definitely started at the bottom of the ladder and with no money. We traveled in a station wagon with a three-week old baby, a five-and-a-half year old, golf clubs, toys, a Crock Pot, a Double Mac and a cooking box. We mostly stayed in Howard Johnson's and shared cookouts with other players while the kids slid down the hills on cardboard boxes. We traveled in caravans communicating with other players via CBs. We timed our travel hours during the oil crunch to coincide with the limited hours the gas stations were open.

> *We traveled in a station wagon with a three-week old baby, a five-and-a-half year old, golf clubs, toys, a Crock Pot, a Double Mac and a cooking box.*

We never thought about being at the bottom. Our goal of building a successful career on the Tour kept us going. Plus we made life-long friends from staying with wonderful people at the tournament sites who welcomed us into their homes. All of us have wonderful memories of these times and feel that these gypsy-type experiences shaped our lives. It all goes back to relationships!

Prior to the Tour, I was a schoolteacher and Doug was a PGA club professional. We were childhood sweethearts (we met at church in the sixth grade). I watched him play high school and college golf, but I never even dreamed about playing the Tour. It was a life I really knew nothing about. Doug, on the other hand, dreamed about it, but never really thought it would be a reality. We both feel truly blessed by the opportunities this career has afforded us, in spite of the ups and downs that came along with it.

— *Pam Tewell*

We don't paint our toenails like the football player on the commercial. We always pretend that Tom is on the back nine. That motivates us both!

— *Martha Jenkins*

I feel that it's important to always be supportive of your husband and never second guess him if he has had a bad day. And try to realize when he needs some private time.

— *K.C. Freeman*

Remember that our feminist strengths may be better used not as the leader of our families, but as the wind beneath the wings of our husbands. It may seem harder to do the work without the glory, but you reap the rewards through a strong marriage and close family.

— *Jennifer McCarron*

I am afraid to think who I would not be, or what would have happened to me as a person and a golfer, if it wasn't for my wife Nicki. She is the determining factor for where I have come from and where I will go. She is the one who gives me the strength and the patience to go on as a human being. After all, life is really the tougher game here, isn't it?

After all, life is really the tougher game here, isn't it?

— *Mike Standly*

Billy is not really superstitious. When we were at a tournament together, he would drive through the gate of the club, and you could just see him preparing himself mentally. The last thing he would always say to me was, "See you later." He never spoke to me until the tournament was over. He has a short attention span. He has to process and program himself a certain way. If anyone disturbs him when he is about to hit the ball, he stops. He puts his club back in his bag, and starts all over again. It's just what he has to do.

— *Shirley Casper*

David Duval has had a profound effect on my husband. Being his father and his teacher, and seeing his success has inspired Bob to play professional golf. The son learned from the father and the father learned to learn from his son. Bob always tells David, "You know I never heard of someone getting shot because they made a double bogey." Move forward in life.

— *Shari Duval*

Frank's father has been his absolute backbone in his career as a professional. His father has helped him financially and emotionally during his Tour career. He always told him that every champion has once failed but continued to try. He said we all must take risks despite the cost if that is the goal we want to reach.

— *Joy Conner*

I think it's important to remember through the highs and lows that our husbands' choice of careers is just that—a job. Like any other profession, some weeks (or years) will be better than others. We will love it more, or less, on any given day. It is a part of our lives— and we respect and honor the game of golf. However, it is not your life. The only ritual I follow is if John is in the lead on Friday, Saturday, or close to it, I never take off and go out to be with him. I just never want to change the pace for him.

— *Suzanne Huston*

I would tell other women to have faith in your husband's career choice because if you don't believe in him, he might have a hard time believing in himself as well. I had two very good friends on tour in the '70s. Whenever they got together, they would talk about how bad this lifestyle was and how sick they were of their husbands playing golf and how they wished they would change jobs. I wouldn't comment. Neither player lasted more than two years on tour and both couples are divorced now. Yes, it would be hard to maintain friendships of other families that don't have to do what we do for a living. But in this day and age, everyone travels a lot, either for business or pleasure and the husband can also have a demanding schedule that will keep him away from home. The only difference is that everyone knows how my husband is doing in his workplace just by looking in the paper. If someone is having a slump in the business world, no one has to know. I just don't think that what my husband does for a living is any big deal. Everyone has to do something. My friends all accept me for what I am just like I would accept them for what goes on in their lives.

The only difference is that everyone knows how my husband is doing in his workplace just by looking in the paper.

— *Jane Adams*

I try to keep things as calm as possible and I have no superstitions. If I really need to talk, I go to the mall and I talk to someone I'll never see again. I work out my problems this way. Everything's worked out, and I don't need to pay a psychiatrist. Loren and I don't dump on each other. Life isn't easy, and neither is marriage. You have to work it out. You can make whatever you want out of a situation.

— *Kim Roberts*

I have been a golfer's wife a long time. My husband John and I started dating at age 14—now 30 years later we're still together. Amaz-

ing. I found out during those years that even though the golfers' wives were a group of diversified women, we were all in the same boat. I think as we age we see how much perseverance we truly have as women and with that, a sense of peace eventually comes in knowing that your patience, faith and courage will see you through anything.

— Kelly Morse

My wife Amy doesn't have any superstitions, but I do. I keep five tees in my right pocket, the same ball repair and ball mark, a quarter and a penny that I have used for years. Then I have this wardrobe thing going. Here it is: There are certain shirts if I've played bad, that won't find their way into the rotation again, ever again. Then there are Friday shirts when I have made the cut; I'm very strange about that. If I miss the cut, then out it goes and it isn't coming with me again. If I need a good round, then I know what shirts are the ones that I've shot 65 in and out they come. Those shirts are always with me.

— Chris DiMarco

I am not superstitious. What happens, happens. But Hal won't play a number two ball. His main caddie Freddie used to tell him, "Whenever you play a number two ball Hal, you don't play as well."

— *Ashley Sutton*

The best motto that I hang onto is, "It is never too late to be what you might have been." And then you have to face the fear head on and do it anyhow. That's what has gotten me through it all. To do this well, you need the support of your spouse; otherwise you are not complete.

— *Tom Jenkins*

I have no rituals or superstitions that I follow regularly. I feel when Tom is still around on Sundays, it's going to be a good week no matter what the outcome of the tournament. I feel it's just another round, even if he is in the lead on Sunday! Tom feels differently.

— *Melissa Lehman*

Jim lets his clubs do the talking! Accomplishments are determined that way. Jim has a passion for pursuing this job. He was and is inspired by his father who has supported and made Jim believe in himself, pushed him. But that changes and it shifts, and then it is the wife who makes those adjustments. I couldn't do what Jim does, or even do it well. He sacrifices a lot in his life. His soul drives him. Jim and I think alike. It's like I am in the same zone with Jim at all times. We are one. If that's a superstition, then so be it, but I get into the same chapter with him. Sometimes, when he is unhappy out there, he'll come over and ask for a hug. Failure is what makes you go forward. You have to learn the failures in order to uncover the successes. Your fears are not what make you quit. You attack your fears and learn to make them an accomplishment.

— *Cyndi Carter*

All that comes to my memory are flashes of experiences—a collage of my life. There have been enough times to have it stand out in my mind that our family has raced through airports, trying to catch planes at the last minute, often with me holding up my pregnant stomach, laughing and saying that we should be on a Hertz Rent-a-Car commercial...I feel like I have spent a year of days packing and unpacking!...We've gotten to visit and enjoy so many beautiful places that many people only dream of visiting!...Still, when you boil it down, the most memorial moments to me on or off the Tour are probably the same as women everywhere: the birth of our children, watching them grow, watching your husband do well after a long dry spell, laughing and story-telling out to dinner somewhere with our whole family, enjoying each other. Lots of miles, lots of hard work, some tears, lots of good times, admiration for fellow Tour families, coming home, lots of phone calls, lots of "I love yous," some weariness, some crankiness, some inconveniences, lots of praying for God's wisdom, memories of traveling in our motor home. We have had ups and downs, and many things have not turned out as I imagined they would. I remember that my dad warned me that you cannot plan out your whole life in advance...

Life moves by so fast and it's so important that we as women, make conscious, wise, selfless choices now, because as sure as anything, we are going to reap what we sow! The power of our influence is so tremendous, either positively or negatively, but there are no replays! There is great hope, though! We can reverse the downward spiral that America's families are on, if we each seek to make a difference. If we do, we will personally and nationally reap such wonderful dividends for generations to come and true fulfillment will come to us—without even having to search for it!

— *Roberta Mast*

For me, lots of personal rituals and superstitions have come and gone. Brian has many more rituals that he follows religiously. I have turned my back during putts, carried crystals, and repeated anything, if it seems to work at the time. But what constantly works comes from within the player. So keeping his mind clear, being positive and helpful is what I tend to do regularly.

— *Cathy Henninger*

I have turned my back during putts, carried crystals, and repeated anything, if it seems to work at the time. But what constantly works comes from within the player. So keeping his mind clear, being positive and helpful is what I tend to do regularly.

I've never set goals because I've already attained so much more in my career than I would have ever done if I set goals. To me the word goal means you stop. My wife says my goal is to beat Tiger Woods. Now that's a heck of a goal. I don't like the word goal because I think when you cross the goal, you stop trying, you stop running. You can always set new goals. Why bother? Why not just go out and do the very best you can and see what develops, what happens? Winning tournaments is a lot of combinations. It's like a crap game. You've got to sit there and throw the dice just right and they have got to bounce right, and you have to get lucky. When you realize that golf is so many good bounces, good breaks, and good shots, it's not always in your control. The bottom line is, whether you're good or bad you're still the one who strikes the ball. It's a fascinating game, a game I've never gotten tired of playing. And as I get older, it's more enjoyable for me.

— *George Archer*

One little thing we always do is talk before Danny plays. No matter what time, he calls before he tees off—always. If I am at the tournament, he always kisses me on the first tee before he begins play.

— *Kimberly Briggs*

I can remember a specific incident a few years back, when I was in Tucson. It was so early in the year, but Mike was really struggling. To top it off, my parents had flown out that week with me. As my dad and I watched Mike hit two consecutive tee balls out of bounds, it was more than I could handle. As we made our way down the fairway and up to the green, I saw Tammy Mayfair waiting to talk to me. She had no idea how bad it was going. Even as supportive as my dad was to Mike and me, he had no idea how really terrible I felt, but Tammy did. When she started asking me how it was going, I completely lost it. She grabbed my arm and pulled me somewhere out of the way. For a minute, I couldn't even form words, but I didn't really have to. Wife to wife, she had been there at some point not too long before that. Anyone else could have walked up that day, and I probably would have held it together, but she was there when I really needed to let it fly. I hope I never have to return the favor, but if she needed it, I'd do exactly the same for her.

Wife to wife, she had been there at some point not too long before that...she was there when I really needed to let it fly.

I am not a superstitious person. Mike can be sometimes, but the superstitions don't seem to last too long. The longest-lasting ritual going is actually still going: He has to have his own comforter and takes it everywhere. He started this the week he won in Greensboro and for the past five years has taken it every week. And believe me he doesn't share it.

— *Crystol Springer*

Bad Hair Days

The key to understanding and coping with life's bumps and grinds, failures and successes, is having a strong support network. Thank goodness venting is allowed.

When my wife and I have a little disagreement, she'll say that's because I played badly. I'll say, "No. I play good. I play bad." I think I'm much more mellow than I used to be. I used to have a lot more fire in the belly. As you get older, you accept things you can't change. You accept bad breaks. Golf is a very strange game. You can hit a perfect drive right down the middle of the fairway and end up in a divot and you can't play. And that's not fair. But that's golf and some days that's going to happen. But the amazing thing is when it's your turn, everything goes your way. That's what you live for.

Golf is a very strange game. You can hit a perfect drive right down the middle of the fairway and end up in a divot and you can't play. And that's not fair. But that's golf and some days that's going to happen.

— *George Archer*

I always tell Ben to focus on the new day. We talk about past accomplishments and our many blessings. It sure makes you thankful for the good times and the successes they have had, and above all else, it teaches you to think positive.

— *Julie Crenshaw*

When David has had a day and I am there, I try to give him some minutes alone before getting together. I then try to be a listener. I search for a positive and try to help him focus on that. I will admit that the early years were not that way. I, too, would feel upset about a bad round. I felt so helpless watching and couldn't understand how it could come out so badly! Neither of us ever won in that emotional situation. Through time and wisdom, I have learned to be supportive and be an encourager and that makes a winning team.

— *Melissa Peoples*

It's funny, you know, with Jack's personality, a bad day means that he would only work harder. And that was the extent of his bad hair day—it enticed him rather than bringing him down. There were several disappointments. I can safely say that Jack never felt badly when someone else won the tournament. He only would feel badly when he lost it. It's that old saying, "Something good comes out of all that bad." Therefore, I have seen a lot of good happen for Jack and for us. He's one of those people that can turn things around. We have always joked that if you are properly prepared, whatever happens, happens. But always know you have done your best. That is the crux of golf.

— *Barbara Nicklaus*

You need to always remind yourself that you are going to have days that are really, really bad. I constantly remind myself this is a sport designed to see that you get beaten, but it's only a game in the purest form of the word.

Here's the interesting thing about golf. You need to always remind yourself that you are going to have days that are really, really bad. I constantly remind myself this is a sport designed to see that you get beaten, but it's only a game in the purest form of the word. If it's your life, then you really have problems.

— *Bob Duval*

To me, I don't believe in moping or whining. It's just like the book *Men Are from Mars, Women Are from Venus.* Fred needs his cave time and I have to stay extremely busy to make it through. The best way I can give Fred support is just to simply stay out of his way! Besides, I don't believe there are mistakes; everything happens for a reason.

— *Thais Couples*

Sure, there are varying stages of tempers and beating up on yourself. Unfortunately, the public has seen me beat the bag or hang some really good cuss words down the stretch. But they don't understand that sometimes the tension becomes overwhelming. It just happens to be in the eye of the public sometimes, and I don't feel great about that. I believe I have a responsibility to be a class act to act professionally, and sometimes, I wish that I wasn't judged. Yes, I am mean to Jim. I expect a lot from him, and sometimes berate him. After all, self-worth in this profession and job is equated with what score I have shot, and we all better know how to move forward from one point to another on any given day.

— *Jim Carter*

I don't say much about a bad day! I just hope Chris gets over it and gets through it. He is pretty good and rarely brings a bad day home with him. If *he* wants to talk about his round then we will. But if he doesn't, we don't.

— *Amy DiMarco*

E very day that we (golfers) go to the golf course, you always have that feeling, "Hey, I could have done better," even if you shoot 64. You always have that unfulfilled feeling when you get off a golf course, no matter how you do, so you try to just hang in there. When you get on the first couple of holes and you make bogeys or even when you're warming up, you know you don't quite have it that day. You just have to approach it and say, "I'll get them tomorrow. I'll just do my best to get through this." That's what the great players do. We all have bad days. The world-class players, the great players, are able to get through those times a lot better than just the guys that are out here making a living. Those guys are able to have that bad day and know they're having a bad day, hang in there and are able to rebound the next day and play great. It's definitely a mental thing and it's every day. You have to work on it every single day of your life and try and prepare for tournaments.

We all have bad days. The world-class players, the great players, are able to get through those times a lot better than just the guys that are out here making a living.

— *David Toms*

W hen Tom has had a bad day he rarely brings it home. But when he does, my reaction is probably different each and every time. Since I'm not a golfer, I have no idea what the pressure to perform must be like. But when Tom is upset about a round and brings it home, we'll talk about it and I listen. I think it's good for Tom to vent his frustration, and I actually don't get upset or embarrassed when Tom shows some negative emotion on the golf course. But on the rare occasions when he gets stuck on something and doesn't go on or get past it, I tell him to quit whining and do better tomorrow.

— *Melissa Lehman*

If Hal has really played well and gotten some bad breaks I tell him that he did great and to keep at it—eventually the putts will drop. He doesn't bring his bad mood home. Our girls help him forget about golf for at least a little while. It is difficult at times because I don't play golf, so I don't have the exact answers for Hal concerning the equipment, courses, yardages, etc. However, I do know how to help him think straighter, to be more positive and focus on the priorities.

— Ashley Sutton

I will have to admit that when John is playing well, I have a better outlook on life. The morning after missing a cut by just one stroke, it is kind of hard to get out of bed and start your day! You have to remind yourself that it is only a game—but it is your husband's career—and that no one died and there is always next week. John is usually fine to be around after a bad day of golf. He doesn't usually take his problems home with him. However, if he is bothered, I'll usually give him some time to let off some steam. If I try to say anything, it's never what he needs to hear anyway. After a while, he'll be okay.

— Jane Adams

When Matt isn't playing well out on the course, I sometimes walk up to him and mumble something random. It could be, "Did you see those baby ducks back there on that par three?" Or, "Look at that airplane." I try to let him know there is more to life than a bad golf shot. I try to get his mind off of the bad. Whatever he does on the golf course doesn't affect our relationship. After he has played and signed his scorecard, I give him a hug and a kiss and tell him that I love him. If nothing else, playing poorly gives you strength and humility for the future. You can draw on those experiences somewhere down the line and hopefully learn from them.

— Blair Gogel

Personally, I'm glad Loren gets mad. It keeps the juices flowing. He'll get mad for 30 minutes or so, or maybe a day and then he'll get on with it. You aren't competitive if you don't express yourself. I on the other hand, don't say anything when Loren has those bad days. I'm not very good with "poor baby." Our kids don't care how well he's done and that helps a  lot. It's not healthy to go on and on about those things. To put things into perspective, Loren's favorite saying is, "When you don't make a cut, it feels like you're being fired from a job."

— Kim Roberts

When things just aren't going right, I just try to stay focused on the fact that it's not going to last forever. I try to work on the fundamentals and sound thinking, and don't get caught up in the panic. That's probably the main thing. As competitors, you know, we have to be totally competitive right this minute and we're all very result-oriented because it's printed in the paper every day. Sometimes you have to get away from being result-oriented and have a goal. You have to realize that maybe your result that day didn't tell the rest of the world that you're headed in the right direction, but, instead, you have to be judged for yourself. You have to be your own judge.

Sometimes you have to get away from being result-oriented and have a goal.

— *Hal Sutton*

When I've had a bad day, or things haven't turned out right, I turn on "SportsCenter," and watch my favorite teams and check in on what they are doing. I take a lot of time to watch the kids do their sports as well—Gigi with her horses and Oliver playing all kinds of sports. That's how I get through a bad week on tour. I especially love to hang out at the barn with my wife and watch her ride the horses.

— *Fred Couples*

I've always said that you can't get down on yourself over one round or even one week. Sometimes there are a few bad weeks before there is a really good one. I am always positive and look at the bright side. I never dwell on a bad day and I tell him the same. Everyone has a bad day at the office. Unfortunately, everyone knows when he does!

— *Lisa Flesch*

Initially, I, too, have feelings of discouragement or at times even despair. But I am not going to allow my feeling to wreak havoc on my life. When Dick has a rough time, I try to allow him some space to rehash his day and let the "sting" wear off. I encourage him to briefly analyze his mistakes and even verbalize them to me. Then I strongly encourage him to immerse himself at home (or with us) and put it aside until tomorrow. Anxiety, disappointment or even disgust and anger are real emotions.

— *Roberta Mast*

> *In years past, my attitude was, "Aw jeez, I missed the cut." Now it's an opportunity to go home. It's totally different.*

I've had quite a few bad days out there at the golf course! Each day's a little bit different. It seems like it's a pretty easy deal when you are playing well, but when you're not, it's frustrating and more difficult. I just keep on working, knowing it's going to get better and change. There's always another tournament next week. In years past, however, my attitude was, "Aw jeez, I missed the cut." Now it's an opportunity to go home. It's totally different.

— *Bob Tway*

Wayne would constantly say after having a bad day that he doesn't belong out here and he can't believe that he could have hit a shot like that. There were three trees out there and he'll ask, "Can you believe that I hit my ball behind one?"

After a few years of listening to this I decided to start agreeing with Wayne. Now he has become much quieter. Now I say to him, "You stink." And then we both smile and laugh!

— *Judy Levi*

I really try to leave it on the golf course. If it's just me I'm going back to, it doesn't matter. But if my kids and Debbye are out with me, I try to do my best and leave all of it at the golf course. When I'm not living up to my expectation, it's difficult. It's quite important to separate the golf with my family time or my poor play could cause problems at home.

— *Brian Watts*

I consider professional golfers to be traveling salesmen; they make a sale and they reap the rewards. Golf is just that way—play well and there's some money. Play bad and you get nothing. The fans and spectators are inspecting everything you do. When things go poorly out there I think to myself, "I'm trying to do my job and I wish you'd leave me alone." But when I'm playing great, I get off on the energy provided by the gallery and everyone who is around. Right now I wouldn't indulge myself when things aren't going my way out on the course. I like the clubs I have, I won't take out a bad day on them! The last time I snapped a club in public was at the 2000 Disney when I had dunked two balls in three holes in the water. I couldn't take it anymore and I immediately felt empowered when I took my 2-iron and ripped it over my bag. What a great feeling! My brother, who was caddying at the time, just laughed. We didn't know until we got to another tournament that the 2-iron was broken. I had snapped the shaft. That was the last time I did that!

— *Bob Heintz*

L et me bring you in on a little secret. I have a bad temper. I best respond to negative feedback, so I take every opportunity to criticize Loren and beat him up when I can, any chance that I can. Then sometimes as I am mumbling to myself even during a tournament round, I'll turn to my caddie and say, "Hey I am the best player in the world." Everyone needs to believe in themselves. Sometimes I have made the worst bonehead shot in golf and think that I am just dogging it, but it makes me fight harder, push farther, and be a better player as a result. What I've learned is how to use negative motivation and make it work for me so I can go forward.

— *Loren Roberts*

W hen Bill has a bad day, I usually just stay quiet until he wants to talk. He never really stays upset for a long time, especially if the kids are there. There are always going to be bad days. Thank goodness there is always tomorrow. This is just something you get used to over time. It becomes your life—bad weeks or bad years come and go, and you have to live through it. Together we always believe in tomorrow, and Bill's ability to bounce back.

— *Courtney Glasson*

Golfers don't commiserate with others. It's a singular sport, and there are different colors to their personalities.

G eorge's body language speaks volumes. However, he was pretty good about not bringing it home, but he could be kind of a brat. My daughters and I dreaded Sunday. We called it "people mover day." If it wasn't a good day for George, I kept the kids quiet. Golfers don't commiserate with others. It's a singular sport, and there are different colors to their personalities.

— *Donna Archer*

Sometimes I don't say very much to Doug because I feel like a broken record and he doesn't want to hear it! But when he is ready to listen, I try to remind him of several things depending on the problem. I remind Doug of the past successes he has had. When he doubts his talent or his place on the Tour, I remind him that if he weren't capable of winning, he wouldn't have kept his Tour card year after year. I also ask him to reflect on the many talented and successful golfers that have gone through periods of problems with their games, bounced back and gotten through it. I always try to remind him that there is more than Doug "the Golfer." It doesn't matter what he does as long as he gives it his best shot.

When he doubts his talent or his place on the Tour, I remind him that if he weren't capable of winning, he wouldn't have kept his Tour card year after year.

— *Leslie Barron*

Hell no! I'm not good to David. I am not very nice to myself, but with age I do see a little patience coming my way. This game of golf is HARD. I remind amateurs that play alongside me of this all the time, and I keep telling myself how hard it is over and over again. Maybe that way I'm off the hook when there are dark days out there, and I have to lighten up. After all, I am human and I am not infallible. Golf is like a big cycle; when you are doing well and playing good, everything tends to get out of whack. Then things start to crumble when you aren't doing well, and you have to get simplified in your life and in your thinking. Spiritually, it softens you. How the big Tour players do it, I'm not sure. It's hard and stressful and the distractions to your function as a human being are out of whack.

— *David Peoples*

Sometimes saying nothing at all is the best thing to do. I've learned that the hard way. Just when you think you've come up with something brilliant, it backfires. I would guess that each player reacts in his own special way. I can tell you that Mike definitely has his "special" way. But when you've been dealing with it for this long, you figure out what you can and cannot say. Or in my case, shouldn't say. I have a hard time NOT addressing behavior that I think might be inappropriate for our younger viewers. Obviously, nothing is ever said during the round, so we can save those conversations for dinner. They are fun. Luckily, by dinner Mike has usually taken his usual "Mad Nap," and has calmed down enough to have a rational conversation. The guy is amazing. He will play the worst round of golf and be absolutely fuming, and what does he want to do? Go take a nap. It's so weird. For myself, I say let's get it all out. Not Mike, he's back in the room snoring.

— *Crystol Springer*

> *When those little smiling faces greet you at the door, you tend to leave the golf at the golf course.*

Dick has always been extremely good about leaving his day at the course. We talk on the phone at least once a day, so by then he's left the course behind. When the children and I did travel with him, I was able to determine when he just needed a little quiet time. I think it was a nice diversion having us there. When those little smiling faces greet you at the door, you tend to leave the golf at the golf course.

— *Joanie Zokol*

Just take the time to be positive. Let him rant, and agree that it's tough. But don't try to understand how he feels because you don't! I try to be as supportive as I possibly can. I will comment to David on all the good shots, focusing on where he succeeded.

— *Molly Sutherland*

Let him rant, and agree that it's tough. But don't try to understand how he feels because you don't!

I am usually the one that is the most upset after a bad day. Tom is real calm on the golf course and off. If his golf game bothers him, he will lie awake at night and worry about it, but he will never, ever take it out on anyone else, except himself. He usually is the one tell-

ing me, "It's okay, Honey. It's only a game." We will go work out, or go off to a movie and get our minds off the day. Nonetheless, it is hard when they have a bad day. They are out there all by themselves solely responsible for making fairly important decisions every ten minutes that can affect their day, their week, or their whole career. That is a lot of pressure.

— *Deb Sieckmann*

When Harrison has had a bad day at the golf course, I try to do several things to make it better. First, I ask very few questions about the round, the missed putts and all the bad shots. I find that it is better to try and find something that Harrison did well that day and remind him of that particular event. I also try to give him enough space to eliminate his steam and shake it off by going to the driving range to hit some balls or to the locker room to think it out. I make an attempt to direct our conversations away from golf and onto something more positive. Most importantly, I remind him that I love him and that he can play great the next day.

— *Allison Frazar*

I am very lucky. Joe doesn't carry the course home with him. I actually have to ask him about his round. I do feel terrible for him when he doesn't have a good day. It actually can depend on your emotions as to how you handle this matter. Sometimes I might say, "What was that?" But I've learned over the years Joe feels bad enough, so I don't make it worse than it already is.

—*Tracey Durant*

I don't overreact to those days that just aren't so good. Jan and I talk about it. I've learned that in the past I've overreacted and tried to make changes when I didn't really need to do anything. Golf is such a fickle game. Try dealing with a hole that's only four and one-half inches wide! A lot of things can happen, so if you talk to other Tour players there will be many times when they're pretty down and out about their game. But all of a sudden, out of the blue, they play a great tournament like David Frost who missed seven or eight cuts in a row, then went on to win in New Orleans one year. That's just golf. You just have to tee it up with the possibility that you can play great golf. If you can't do that, then you should go home.

Golf is such a fickle game. Try dealing with a hole that's only four and one-half inches wide!

— *Larry Rinker*

Even though he won't talk about a bad round or seem bothered by it, he thinks about it for a long time afterward. I know that golf is on his mind pretty much 24/7.

Because Cam is so laid back, he's not one to be in a terrible mood for too long after a bad round. I feel really lucky here because I've heard that some of the guys are very irritated for a long time after a round and withdraw from their wife or girlfriend. After a bad round, I don't initiate a lot of conversation and I never ask questions about what happened out on the golf course until Cam wants to talk about it. I just give him a hug and a kiss, and let him talk when he is ready. One thing I do know for sure is that even though he won't talk about a bad round or seem bothered by it, he thinks about it for a long time afterward. I know that golf is on his mind pretty much 24/7.

— *Jennifer Beckman*

I always found that if I did have a bad time out on the golf course, at least I was very, very consistent. Usually when I had a bad tournament or bad times, it was because I was mentally worn out from playing too much. And I realized I had to get away. I would get away for a period of time, and I was always able to recognize that. I'd go home and Shirley would allow me to go fishing. She realized that was my release, so I'd go out and spend a night on the ocean, fish the next day and come back. Maybe I'd be home for two or three weeks, and maybe fish five or six times and that was great therapy. I didn't have to go and talk to someone like a counselor. I just went out and thought about the fish.

— *Billy Casper*

Oh well! I listen and after a while there is not much more to say. If I wasn't at the tournament and saw it on TV, I highlight what Chip did right. About four years ago my husband missed a cut by shooting a 77 that day, and when he came home, our daughter Mary Catherine asked her daddy to give her a bath. Chip told her that he had had a bad day, and at six she asked him, "Daddy, how do you have a bad day?" If only we could think like a child!

— *Karen Beck*

Honestly, my responses usually reflect my day! How I am feeling. If Danny has been gone three weeks, missed three cuts, the five children are all fighting, and I am feeling lonely, I may not have a kind response. My frustrations sometimes creep through and Danny is usually the one who ends up encouraging me. However, on a good day I listen hole by hole, shot by shot, from the first tee to the very last putt. Every detail is expressed. I always express my love for Danny and my sincere belief in what he is capable of doing. I remind him that it is possible to shoot a 75 after a day shooting a 64 on the course, and the same holds true in reverse. Anything is possible in this game. You don't know what the next day holds for you.

Anything is possible in this game. You don't know what the next day holds for you.

— *Kimberly Briggs*

I always try to encourage Duffy if it's a bad day. After all, a golf tournament can change for you when the birdie putts start falling in. You never know when that might happen, so it's important to stay positive and look ahead. If I am not with Duffy at a particular tournament and he calls, I listen and try to sense if he is looking for suggestions or just needs a good listener. Golf is only a part of our lives, and you can't focus on it all of the time, just like any occupation.

— *Vicky Waldorf*

For the first few years I didn't do well at this, because I caddied most of the time for Kenny. I, too, would feel like a failure and then we'd both need lifting up! As we grew together and Kenny would share what he *needs* from me, I was able to give him that reassuring hug of love and remind him of who has a bigger and better plan if we continue to persevere through the valleys.

— *Karen Knox*

O ut there on tour, all these guys are working really hard, and fighting to keep their Tour cards. I truly hope that everyone plays well and the first thought in my heart is that my husband Jay Don wins. After all, he is trying his best and working so hard. I don't think about the Donna Karan belt that I could buy after my husband makes a putt. Jay Don is thinking about how he can help everyone else if he wins something. He has so much love and goodness

in his heart. I used to joke with the media, and would tell them that I don't play golf because we can't have two professionals in the family—this is the hardest game in the world to play! Jay Don doesn't bring home his emotions, but I am ready to call the President! He's so even-keeled—he could have the worst day out there, and then asks me where are we going for dinner. Jay Don's favorite saying is, "You never know with golf." Yet I wonder why doesn't it happen out there, and why doesn't it happen more often for him?

— *Marci Blake*

I remember a time just before Texas when I was really playing rotten and yet I was kind of getting away with it out on the course. I played rotten the week before, and I decided to come home and do nothing. I call that a cleansing. I try to forget everything I've been working on for the last few months in two days. I try to erase the whole chalkboard and start over. When I'm having one of those bad golf days, I just stop and forget about it, and start over. Sometimes I can't change what's happened, but in those cases like Texas, I felt like I got all of it out of my system and started new, went down there and almost won.

— *Mark Wiebe*

My wife doesn't think I beat myself up enough, that I just accept things. But inside, I don't. I just don't show them. I am pretty emotionless. I don't run around and do a high-five if I have a birdie, but I might bang a club if I hit a bad one. It eats at you, but I don't try to show it too much because I know too much emotion one way or another can maybe hurt you even more. Deep down it hurts me if I don't do as well as I want and I just don't show it. I think that's where Laura might not understand me as well. I tell her I'm dying inside, but I don't want to take it out on her or the kids.

— *Bradley Hughes*

It eats at you, but I don't try to show it too much because I know too much emotion one way or another can maybe hurt you even more.

After we had our first two daughters, Mike's bad days were lessened. The importance of a poor day seemed to be not so all encompassing. When I would pick our girls up from the nursery, the first thing they'd say after running to me was, "How did Dad play?" As if it made a difference. These children were and are so much more important than the putts that didn't drop. This doesn't mean that he walks off the golf course always smiling and happy after a tough day, but we give Mike the time to process and evaluate. Then we discuss how we can help him achieve the balance we are all working for.

— *Randolyn Reid*

I can't have bad hair days, because I have no hair! Golf is not a life-or-death event in our lives. I know I am going to have bad rounds, and my whole attitude is that if I can't have fun doing this, then I have no business being out there on the Tour. I can see that in the first part of the Tour year, I am fresh and my attitude is good, and I have patience. But as it gets late in the season, coupled with all the travel, you get tired and when that happens, your attitude gets negative and it's  time to regroup and take a breath. It's a waste of time to get depressed. This is really just a game—period.

— *Tom Jenkins*

Riding the Roller Coaster
...and Holding On

Unfortunately, inconsistency and uncertainty comprise the many facets of life no one can avoid; however, this is reality.

There are ups and downs and there are the dry spells when nothing goes right. Then it turns around and it seems that all the putts drop. Maintaining a really positive attitude during those down times can be a chore.

Bob was a club pro all his career. He tried qualifying for the Senior Tour at age 50 and got a conditional card and fell right into his element. Sometimes you do get a second chance. When he was out with an injury, we regrouped and planned for the next year. In essence, there are highs and lows. But if we only get to fulfill his dream for three years, we would have no regrets. Some people never get the chance. We now set new goals—and we will achieve them.

— *Shari Duval*

Russ and I have been together since grade school. Our First Communion pictures were together. We were always in love, even when someone else brought me Valentine candy. When we started out, Russ had to borrow money from his uncle to go down and play on the Space Coast Tour. And when he got his card in 1981, we were really down to maybe $5,000 and I was pregnant with Ryan. At one time we even stayed in a hotel with bars on the windows and soap that was used and abused. When Russ won his first tournament, the excitement was unbelievable. While his career hasn't been tops all the time, we say he has done well. He has brought the diapers home and we are just fine now!

— *Jackie Cochran*

When he got his card in 1981, we were really down to maybe $5,000 and I was pregnant with Ryan. At one time we even stayed in a hotel with bars on the windows and soap that was used and abused.

Doug played on the Nike Tour and the mini-tours for almost four years before getting his PGA Tour card. After three or four tries at the final stage of Tour school, sometimes the PGA seemed unattainable. It would always be a disappointment, but then again it isn't something that you can expect. To get your card is more than half the battle. Truthfully, some of the best times we have had together have been on the mini-tours driving through the country instead of flying. We didn't have any money and had a very full life and lots of first-time experiences.

— Leslie Barron

As an amateur tournament player myself, I understand the ups and downs of being a competitive golfer. Robin, has been making the climb uphill at a steady rise. Once his "work" is completed, Robin is able to switch back to the husband/father role in the time it takes for him to change shoes and meet at the car. If he has a bad day, I have found the less I say, the better. I realize he feels a hell of a lot  worse about his day than I do and we both know how any given day this sport can change from shooting a 74 one day to a 64 the next.

— K.C. Freeman

M att and I have been through some very exciting times together (wins, travels, etc.) as well as some very difficult ones (losses, Q-school, etc.) over the last eight years. From these experiences I have learned a great deal, most importantly, not to let the lows get too low and the highs too high. This philosophy is as simple as a birdie streak or as complicated as a major slump. Learning not to let my emotions swing so drastically is what keeps me sane. One week he can win, and the next miss the cut. This is the beauty of pro golf. Things can turn around so quickly that you learn never to enjoy the moment too much as well as not to let each other get too down during the tough times. It only takes one shot to turn it around. Advice? Embrace both the bad and good. If you embrace your feelings of fear and disappointment, they will only make you stronger.

Embrace both the bad and good. If you embrace your feelings of fear and disappointment, they will only make you stronger.

— *Blair Gogel*

S teve is seven years older than I am, and therefore he went through a lot of struggles in golf before he even knew me. He had been through Qualifying School several times, and had been on and off the Tour. He had also played in several mini-tours. When we met, he was about to go to Qualifying School, and I really did not have a clue about the PGA Tour or golf! I thought this was normal and easy for him. At that time, he had won about $15,000, which was almost as much as my dad made in a single year. I liked this guy! Steve's golf career was like a stepladder. After that, he began to play better. But I am familiar with injuries that can sideline a golfer. These injuries have given us time to reflect and strengthen our relationships with each other and our children.

— *Bonnie Jones*

> *What I truly believe is that my husband is one of the most talented guys in the world and he has the talent to win every week or be in contention every week.*

In the past years that I have been out here with Billy on Tour, we have seen it all and it is absolutely mind-boggling. The highs are so high and the lows are so low. And trying to figure out how to keep it on an even keel is the part of the challenge I love. It's interesting to learn how to handle all the different situations and the challenges that come about. We have really had some roller coaster years. What I truly believe is that my husband is one of the most talented guys in the world and he has the talent to win every week or be in contention every week. It's the mental challenges that we go through together that make you strong. You can't be at your best every day at the office, but yet, every time he steps inside the ropes to play, he is ready to be a player. I am just as frustrated when he isn't reaping the rewards from all his hard work. Yet I know he can—and I'll always be there. I try to find the positive side of each experience, so that together we learn how to move forward.

— *Tammy Mayfair*

Learning to handle the ups and downs of Tour life is the biggest hurdle for a wife. It took several years for me not to "live and die" with every shot Doug made. But I realize that those shots were for our livelihood—food, clothing and shelter. If "we" missed the cut (and Doug and I have always considered ourselves a team), there was simply no paycheck that week. The uncertainty of that was stressful, to say the least! But at the same time, I know it has made us stronger and certainly more appreciative and grateful for the really good times we are having on the Champions Tour.

— *Pam Tewell*

At one point we drove a Volvo around the country chasing our dream with Rachael, our daughter, who was a baby at the time in 1989-90. We had all our belongings in that car and I played in the Hogan Tour. It was one of our things; if we were going to play golf, we were going to do it together. Melissa and I didn't get married for her to work at Nordstroms and for us to be apart, and if we ever got to the point when I could not support her or our family, then it was our agreement that I would quit.

— *Tom Lehman*

Because Duffy and I have been together since I was just 15 years old, I have never experienced anything else but what revolves around golf. I find that a firm belief in him and his abilities have given us both strength. The one thing that I knew throughout his college career was once he was comfortable he became more confident. In his senior

year at UCLA, he was NCAA Player of the Year. Duffy has since continued to improve as he matures. His first five years on tour were slow. He had to go back to qualifying school four out of those five years, but once he went for his fifth time, he has maintained his presence on the PGA Tour. Now, after many years on tour, and with victories in 1999 and 2000—he is well on his way. But even with that, the hardest part for Duffy has been for him to always have the same belief in his own ability that his coaches, family and friends know he has.

— *Vicky Waldorf*

I stopped playing golf for a period of fifteen months between 1995 and 1997 after Nancy and I had our first child. Things weren't going too well. My friend and Yale coach, Dave Peterson, came for Christmas dinner and when he walked into our home, without even saying hello to me said, "Bob, you look like shit!" (I was topping 235 pounds.) "Why aren't you playing golf?" I told Dave I had no money and barely could afford the roof over our heads. "My God, man." Dave said. "Don't you remember where you went to school? If you need money, I'll get you the money. Just ask me." Well, I got the money and went off to the Hooters Tour and killed them in 1998. All the Yale guys who put up the money for me got a kick out of it. They were making a lot of money. It was as if they had a horse in the race again. While the Hooters Tour bonus program would provide me with a guaranteed weekly salary, I opted for using my conditional Nike card that I had earned. I didn't turn professional to spend one more year on "The Hooters." Even my mom tried to convince me to play where the money would come in weekly. She still cries about it when she thinks that she tried to influence me to take the safe route. Considering I had a degree in economics from Yale, I knew better. Talk about a major suck-up by a wife—Nancy gave up what we called home, packed up all our belongings, put them in storage and either lived with me out of a van while I toured, or moved in with my parents. She made a big sacrifice. Right off the bat, I went out and won the first Nike event and went on to acquire my Tour card.

Nancy gave up what we called home, packed up all our belongings, put them in storage and either lived with me out of a van while I toured, or moved in with my parents. She made a big sacrifice.

— *Bob Heintz*

Having a healthy happy marriage and fun, good-behaving kids is what it's all about. You realize you can get through it all by sticking together and not losing focus on the bigger picture of life. The most difficult part of it all is not knowing what to say. Sometimes you just feel like screaming at David and saying, "Hey, what was all that about?" But you know that he hasn't played like that on purpose, so you can't use that approach! Sometimes, you just get tired of being a cheerleader. They don't want to hear that either, so you give them their space for 30 minutes or so, and then life goes on. Sometimes it is best to just be there and remain silent.

— *Sharon Ogrin*

The most difficult part of being the wife of a professional golfer is the financial instability. It's scary to know that you may or may not get your job back the next year, unless of course you win. But even with a win, unless it's a major, it's only good for two years. I'm playing it safe; I am the kind of save-money person. When we've made some big financial decisions that I know will increase our monthly expenses, it makes me nervous because I want to make sure that we can still handle everything if Cam is not making much money. You don't know how long good or bad playing phases are going to last!

— *Jennifer Beckman*

Our relationship spanned over 50 years, and I never called him Gene; it was always Mr. Selvage. It was a matter of respect. He was a great role model for me.

I had a few people who wanted to sponsor me as a professional golfer. One group was a bunch of newspapermen in San Francisco, but they really couldn't afford it. If I had not been successful, I would have felt badly if they lost money on me. But a gentleman named Mr. Selvage said he wanted to sponsor me. I had known him since childhood when I caddied for him. He had just bought a bull for $50,000, who turned out to not like cows! So I figured, if he could buy a $50,000 bull, I wasn't going to lose any sleep over losing money for him. I felt that this was the right kind of partnership I wanted to enter into. He was an amazing man, and treated me like I was his own son. He didn't have a son and liked how I respected him. We would go hunting together and played golf together. We stayed friends all through his life, and we had a very special relationship. He had two daughters like Donna and me, and he said right from the start that he wasn't doing this to make money, but to help me. My own daughter, who is a pastor, buried him when he was 98 years old and we remained close friends right up until his death. Our relationship spanned over 50 years, and I never called him Gene; it was always Mr. Selvage. It was a matter of respect. He was a great role model for me.

— *George Archer*

L et's face it, golf is a game about peaks and valleys, and it requires me to be true and honest with myself. Being disqualified at Tour school is a fine example of a downer. But it happened. Then I go down to Mexico for a Nike event, and it's coming down to the last hole with Mike Donald and I realize things aren't going really well. When you miss a couple of cuts, that doesn't exactly build confidence. I found out that it is normal to hit bottom and then come back up. I can get frustrated. What you have to do is build momentum and mean it! Building that throughout the week and hitting your stride on Saturday and Sunday sets your tone as a golfer. After all, you need to look at the winners of tournaments. They have built on their games from the week before. That's what I generally strive for. Golf defines who you are, and what you will choose to do with that. I guess you could say that would be my personal motto for my job and my life.

When you miss a couple of cuts, that doesn't exactly build confidence. I found out that it is normal to hit bottom and then come back up.

— *Matt Gogel*

B eing away from each other for long stretches can define the pure pressure and just that can bring about the highs and lows. I try my best to keep Fuzzy's mind off golf and away from all that when he is off the course. My motto for him is, "Outta sight, outta mind!" I believe, as I have told Fuzzy, that today is over so let's try and make tomorrow a better one. After all, you can't fix whatever has happened—it's over.

Today is over so let's try and make tomorrow a better one.

— *Diane Zoeller*

After college graduation, I worked as a bag boy for almost five years at a country club in San Luis Obispo. The tips that I received were dear, and the time we had on the course was something to be cherished after everyone in the club left. A bunch of us would get together and play for five bucks. It was the staff against the pros and assistant pros. One day I went out with the assistant pro and I finally beat him. I couldn't believe it, and it was only because of my putting. As he was handing me the five big ones, he turned and said to me, "Loren, if you couldn't putt, you couldn't play golf worth a lick." This comment always stuck with me. I am a good putter, am I not? Look at the statistics!

— Loren Roberts

I take one tournament at a time; Dick and I deal with the players at one time or another have struggles of some sort. When Dick is playing, I follow the scores on the Internet as much as possible. But that is difficult because you really have no idea how they are playing other than just seeing the numbers on the computer. Talk about nerve-racking—while Dick may be playing well, he could have a bad break on a hole or two and it could mean missing the cut. Dick has incredible patience, which you must have in order to persevere.

— Joanie Zokol

When we were first married, Bob wasn't on the Tour so we played in state opens and mini-tour events all over the country. I remember feeling quite useless in the early years because all I did was follow him around and support him. I tried to think of something I could do that was rewarding and possible while traveling all the time. I never found it, but maybe those early years made me stronger and able to handle all of life's details later.

I will never forget how I felt when Bob won the 1986 PGA Championship in Toledo, Ohio. He was playing the final round, four shots in back of Greg Norman at the start of the day. He chipped in from the bunker on the 18th hole to go ahead by one and win his first and only major to date. When the tournament officials gave Bob the trophy, he was fine until he saw my tears, then he cried, too. It sometimes looks wimpy to cry over a golf tournament, but until you've gone through the emotional roller coaster of a tight final round of a major tournament and suddenly—ka-boom!— you hole out of a bunker, well, let's see how you would do.

— *Tammy Tway*

A Tour wife is supportive of her husband throughout the good and the bad. It's very frustrating at this level, not knowing if my husband Chris, or anyone's husband out there on Tour, will have a job from year to year. Missed cuts add up, confidence goes down, and my job is supposed be to remain stable, calm and reassuring!

— *Morgan Couch*

The most difficult part of being the wife of a professional golfer was not really being able to plan ahead—like a budget. Unlike other professional sports with guaranteed salaries and per diems, with golf, you earn whatever you earn by performance only.

— *Karen Knox*

I took two MBA courses in the business sector in graduate school, thinking I would pursue this. But I was dismayed and uninspired, to say the least. I learned that if these people were serious about business, then I could be more serious about something I really loved.

I yearned to be a professional golfer. And that experience enlightened me. I learned that there really wasn't much to turning professional as a golfer. Just walk right up, sign in at qualifying, and you must be flat broke to do so! That's the scenario for most of us. There really isn't much to turning pro. Well, I learned quickly. I missed Qualifying School, where my roommate was Duffy Waldorf, during my first attempt to qualify in Greenleaf, Florida. Every night Duff would have a pint of Haagen-Dazs vanilla ice cream, and my wife, Cyndi, remembers this as his good-luck dessert! The options ahead were to play in Asia and on the mini-tours out and around the Southwest, Arizona and Utah. In 1986 I spent three months in Asia, and that experience taught me how to be a pro. I learned what a diversified group we are as golfers. The European players played differently; they putted in such a great way on greens that, if measured, would be a three on the stimp meter. It's not that they had great skills, but rather they learned to play with what was there for them, and it was clear that those golfers knew it was a job of imperfections. They put up with more, and they are less cluttered in their thoughts of perfecting techniques. They focused on just being great players. The conditions in Asia make the American professional golfer crawl and their skin quiver. But not these guys. Once I remember walking on the course without a golf club and a snake did a belly flop like a 180-pound man. The hair stood up on my body and stayed in that position until I got back to the driving range. But the cultural differences and exposure opened my eyes and sharpened me. I am much more patient as a result now.

— *Jim Carter*

Hey—this life isn't normal. There aren't paychecks every Friday. It used to be that I would get in Mike's face—try to be funny, or just plain back off. Now I attempt to ask and communicate in such a way that he can express himself freely, and I am a better listener. Together, what we have been through as a couple, and the profound impact of Payne Stewart's death, have changed the way we look

and approach things. I will tell the kids the truth—your father had a bad day—and let them come up with what they need to do or say to their father. He used to get depressed, question his self-worth, or be consumed with anger. Now, he has matured and gone through a metamorphosis. The key for any intimate relationship is to express yourself and take inventory. If you make the effort to make the changes, then it will happen.

— Nicole Standly

Tour daycare is my lifesaver. Traveling with the Tour takes its toll, especially on the kids. But being home alone for weeks at a time does, too. So is it better to be tired and cranky together (with Daddy) or lonely at home? Packing and unpacking for myself and the children, making sure we have enough snacks and entertainment for our travel days, living out of suitcases and duffel bags, finding ways to do the laundry, travel-size shampoos, trying to stay organized, making sure the bills are paid—these are the day-to-day tasks. It's sometimes hard to keep track of the day of the week and the city we are in from one week to the next.

— Nancy Heintz

When I first got on the Tour, each week I didn't know what to expect. I didn't know much about the tournaments, and I was just trying to get by and survive and keep my Tour card. I wanted to have some job security for the next year. But then, the last few years as I started to win, and have had more success, I just look forward to competing more every week. Before that, I was trying to just get by. Kind of thinking all the time, can I do this or can I not do this? Now I know I can and it's a lot more enjoyable. I have some job security. I can go out and try to play to win. I approach tournaments a lot differently than I used to. I've played as many as 31 tournaments in one year, and will do so until my son reaches school age. When he can't come out as much, then I know I'll cut back. I want to get my game to the point where I can play fewer tournaments and still finish high on the money list. It will take more work and better play, but I look forward to the challenge.

— *David Toms*

Handling the roller-coaster rides of the Tour can be emotionally draining. I try, through my faith in God, to keep golf in perspective. I am human and find as I watch a round of golf either live or via the Internet, my emotions can go all over the map. I keep focused in my mind that David is doing the very best he can with each shot or situation.

— *Melissa Peoples*

Before we were on the PGA Tour, chasing other tours to play on. We had very little if any money at all, but we did have each other and the ability to enjoy ourselves. There were several times when Tom considered giving up, and we would think long and hard if this is what we should be doing with our lives. When faced with this question, there were always two points that I would add to the equation. I would ask, "Is Tom having fun, or does he really hate this?" And, "Are we going to starve if we continue this?" At those times, our faith in God, my personal faith in Tom's abilities in golf, and our faith in each other would help us reach the same conclusion: Let's do this because we are still having fun and we've never gone hungry. And now as I look back and reflect, everything has pieced itself together, and we face the challenges that lie ahead. I'm so grateful for the way we started out together—the lessons that we learned, and still learn, on and off the Tour.

— Melissa Lehman

Scott started out on the mini-tours and then made it through Q-School on his third try—straight from the Hooters Tour! We had no idea what we were in for on the PGA. I agreed to quit my job and travel with him. We used money put up for us by guys who loved golf and wanted to sponsor Scott. We were broke—and actually in debt. Scott tells people, "When I told her that I wanted to quit my job and play golf, she said, 'Okay.' I still can't believe that she did!" But I don't honestly think it took strength so much, just trust and the carefree nature of young adulthood. We didn't have much to lose!

— Jennifer McCarron

Together we have been through many bad days! I would have to say, however, that a lot of sacrifices have been on Jim's part. And through that, you have to find a balance in your heart. Communication is the key, after all. Jim says that I am the only person that he can trust with his deepest feelings. Every day that Jim tees it up, he bares his soul—he is judged each time. As his wife, I am his partner and his sounding board. Before Jim won in Tucson after 14 years out there on tour, he would always question himself and ask, "When am I going to win? When is this going to happen to me?" Or, "Am I ever going to win?"

And I would say to him, "There are all those tournaments out there to take a shot at and I believe there is always an opportunity to step up to the plate and walk home with the hardware."

When Jim finally did win, he commented that the other players embraced him and gave him congratulatory hugs and well wishes expressing how proud they were. For Jim, and for all the players out there, this is how you define the companionship among the Tour players. When things go wrong, I can hear it in Jim's voice—that sense of doubt. In a supportive way, I tell him that he needs to continue to believe he belongs out there on the PGA Tour. I pretty much am blunt and tough and comment that he has worked his rear end off and I don't want to hear that you question where you belong.

When Jim finally did win, the other players embraced him and gave him congratulatory hugs and well wishes expressing how proud they were. For Jim, and for all the players out there, this is how you define the companionship among the Tour players.

— *Cyndi Carter*

W hen I started out playing golf, my first goal was winning money. Both of us came from families with little money. Shirley and I married in 1952, and met when I was a senior and she was a sophomore in high school. We lived on $77.50 every month, and I made $54.58 every two weeks. She worked in a department store and did this for four years.

I was in the Navy from 1951-55. In April of 1954, I became a professional golfer while in the service, and at the end of 1955 we went out on tour. My sponsor gave me $650 per month and we bought a trailer and a car. I had to give them 30 percent and pay the money back. After three years we went on our own! In the late '70s, when I was older, things started going down. I was beginning to get a few years on me and that was about the times things started sliding as far as my career was concerned. We moved to Utah, and I got into a big land deal that went kaput. We were building a large house at the same time. We had a lot of troubles financially. But we got through it. We had a great attorney. Shirley was right there all the time doing things. To keep it all going, she had garage sales. Shirley was ingenious at keeping us afloat.

— Billy Casper

I am a realist! I know it is possible to lose your game or lose interest in the game of golf. Not that I'm a worrier, but it happens. Lisa is my strong suit and keeps me grounded. My wife keeps me believing in my ability even when I miss cuts one after another. As a professional golfer, I know sometimes we take for granted how well we are treated. There aren't many sports where the spectators can get as close to the athletes as they do in golf. That's one of the redeeming qualities of golf and I feel like a journeyman.

— *Steve Flesch*

When Glen and I first met, I had to buy dinner. We did not start out with a lot. We spent three years in Europe on tour, which is much more fun now to look back on it than it was at the time. We both had high hopes and I never doubted Glen's abilities. No one could ever say that I married Glen for his money, but rather his good looks and redneck personality!! I had really expected to marry someone with a nine-to-five job. But because I had grown up with my dad being a club pro, I knew what it meant to miss traditional holidays together as a family, and to have awkward schedules. I do feel that prepared me for what life had in store. I try to remember, when the pressure gets to be too much, that I really would not want anything to change. So I expect the peaks and valleys that come with this package. It's not to say that I don't get goose bumps when Glen makes an eagle and on the same note, I dread when we play bad. Somehow, we look at each other and remind ourselves…Golf is just a game.

— *Jennifer Ralston-Day*

I really don't feel like I am that old in my forties. I still feel competitive and can play the game well enough to win. Yes, it's been a long and frustrating dry spell to get over that hump. But every year I set goals to win multiples. Trying to achieve those goals, I re-dedicate my focus and keep working hard. I try to have a good, positive attitude. After all, you can't force it to happen—it's all about management, and if I'm not happy off the golf course, then I won't be happy there playing on the course. That's the whole package. The ups and downs of golf can give you the greatest high ever, and it's an accomplishment to even get there on Tour. My dream is always to win, and reach a level that I can play. Sure, there are frustrations and disappointments, but they are all learning experiences. One shot can make all the difference, even when you are struggling so hard and down on yourself. And then in a split second, you can hit more than a mediocre shot and your whole attitude turns around.

— *Jay Don Blake*

P rior to my first pro tournament victory at the Hong Kong Open in February of 1993, I almost quit playing. This got me going. It gave me a lot of confidence. I built on this win and took advantage of it. Prior to 1998, I had won several tournaments in Japan, and I realized I could play to my ability if given the opportunities on Tour. I had played well, but never let it happen—I was trying too hard. In 1998, I was runner-up at the British Open, and as a result, I got my PGA Tour card for 1999. Thankfully, I didn't have to go to Qualifying School, which I had only previously made one time.

— *Brian Watts*

Handling the ups and downs on Tour is the best way to build your character. That's the way I like to view it. How we face each situation that comes about says a lot about us as people. For me, it's taken awhile to be comfortable in dealing with every situation. Mike and I married in September 1989. In January 1990, I quit my job, packed up everything we owned (which wasn't very much), bought a van and took off. He won the inaugural Ben Hogan event and with the first-place money we were off and running. My contribution that year was carrying his bag. What an experience that was. If you can caddie for your husband, you can get through *anything* together! We fought over the typical stuff, like he always had too much crap in that bag. Give me a break— when it's 90 degrees outside, do you really

> *If you can caddie for your husband, you can get through* anything *together!*

need a rain suit in there? That year was a typical one for us. Missed three cuts, placed third in an event, missed two cuts, finished in the top ten, missed four cuts and then he WON! When it came down to the last three weeks, he knew he had to win two out of the last three to be exempt for the PGA Tour. The next week Mike went out and did exactly that. Now we were really on our way.

> *The players that experience the rise and fall will always come out with a little more character because they have passed the test.*

In 1991 there we were on the Big Tour—everything we dreamed of. Mike handled the transition like he does everything else, BALLS OUT! We can look back and laugh. He had no problem keeping his exempt status for three years, and in 1994 he sprung loose. That year he managed to become the first American on the Tour to be a two-time winner. We were lovin' it.

During 1994, Mike lost his long-time teacher Ralph Lomeli, and he was devastated. Things started to break down and there was no one to fix it. It's been an up-and-down struggle, even after establishing a new teacher and a new swing. We are waiting for that long-awaited door to open. This has been a personal growth period for us. It has been extremely difficult for me to deal with the fact that when things go badly, there's no sign of them getting better. It's hard not to play off your spouse's disposition. Mike gets SO frustrated and so do I. That's the plight of being a wife. Mike has to be at peace with himself to get back to the level that he enjoys. After all, you can't play for your friends, your family, not even for your wife and kids. The players that experience the rise and fall will always come out with a little more character because they have passed the test. Determination!!! I now know my strength comes from acceptance. I appreciate Mike's determination and he appreciates my dedication to him and our kids. We gather the strength from each other, knowing that all of our sacrifices will be rewarded.

That's the plight of being a wife. Mike has to be at peace with himself to get back to the level that he enjoys. After all, you can't play for your friends, your family, not even for your wife and kids.

— *Crystol Springer*

G olf, like life, has its ups and downs. You learn to embrace the "ups" and accept the "downs" as they come. After all, tomorrow is another day, and next week is another opportunity to win or play at your best.

— *Jan Rinker*

M y big thing is money, and being afraid to not be able to pay bills. It scares me. When Joe first started playing, we actually lived from paycheck to paycheck. But in the long run, it has helped us because we remember what it was like to have no money and we appreciate what we have. There have been many times that I felt that I could help Joe out there on the course, being a golfer myself, but I have learned over the years to just let it go, and be there for him when

he is done. I am probably more nervous when he plays well than when he doesn't. As we experience this together, I sit back and realize that those days back on the mini-tours or in 1993 when Joe got his card, we didn't understand the bigger picture. As a matter of fact, Joe quit golf after that year and sold insurance. That was awful. I don't think that he sold even one policy. I convinced Joe to go back out and play in the Nike Tour where I caddied for him and each and every year he got better and better. He actually felt like he belonged out there and I did too. In 1996, Joe finished third on the Nike Tour and off we were to the PGA.

— *Tracey Durant*

When I met Danny he was on the PGA Tour. I never had heard of "Q-School." Our first year of marriage was just traveling from one beautiful place on tour to the next, but at the end of that first year, Danny just missed keeping his Tour card—and off we went to Q-School. There he missed qualifying to get his card back by just one shot. I had no idea what that meant, nor did I know the journey we were about to begin. After all, at that time there was no Nike or Hogan Tour to fall back on. Lots of things were taking place in our life all at one time—we had just moved to Arizona, had a baby, and Hogan cancelled his club deal. And, the TPC of Scottsdale did not give Danny playing privileges that year. Talk about everything happening at once! Together we have gone through growth periods, but it seems that everything has a way of working out. One year again and Danny missed getting his Tour card by one shot—he was devastated—but two days later we found out that we were expecting twins. To put it straight, I really needed him to be closer to home. At that time Danny ended up playing some events and then landed a TV show. It was the best year! But I will never forget the year that Steve Jones called the day after Q-School when Danny had missed again. I began to express my pain and frustration to Steve, and he said, "God gave Danny a talent, but that doesn't mean he will be the PGA Player of the Year right now—He (God) will place him where he is needed and then maybe someday Danny will be where he wants to be." It's plain and simple—not everyone gets to be a PGA star. But, if you have an opportunity to make a living doing what you love and fulfilling your passion, then you are truly lucky.

It's plain and simple—not everyone gets to be a PGA star. But, if you have an opportunity to make a living doing what you love and fulfilling your passion, then you are truly lucky.

— *Kimberly Briggs*

Tom and I started dating in 1983. His parents gave me a crash course on birdies and bogeys because I knew nothing about golf. I was an R.N. and then went into modeling professionally. We married in 1989. I can remember how difficult it was to accept the weekly highs and lows, watching Tom out there. He used a three-ball putter and then an "H" shaped Star Fighter putter. One day, as I walked in the gallery outside the ropes, I had to endure the spectators' negative and sarcastic comments like, "What's he using? A rake? A TV antenna? I've never seen anything so ridiculous." On and on. Everyone thought they were the expert and I was ready to take a golf club myself and start swinging at every one of them. I can remember being reduced to tears a few times, but I learned to shake it off. It was a learning experience for me and gave me the strength to support my husband out there. Together we enjoyed ten years out on tour and when our first baby was born who had some health problems, Tom began to think long and hard about the future and his family. Although he got involved in the money-making part of it, golf was not fun anymore. Being away from the family compounded this feeling. He was plagued with neck problems that led to missed cuts and losing his Tour card. He's been through Tour school several times since. We've been at the bottom, the middle and the top in his career. I support him all the way in whatever he decides to do. I know he has it within himself to make things happen and to do what he needs to do. You have to be strong to make it over the hurdles that life gives you.

> *I can remember being reduced to tears a few times, but I learned to shake it off. It was a learning experience for me and gave me the strength to support my husband out there.*

— *Deb Sieckmann*

People think that golf is all about the glamor and it's easy to do since the public hears what they get paid and all the perks, but it's not. No matter what, outsiders don't have a clue. When your husband hits a ball into the trees, it's painful. Outsiders may think it isn't a big deal, but it is a big deal—there is Jay Don thinking about what he is doing now at this particular moment in time, not what is to come. I often wonder what side of the ropes the spectators are on. They don't understand the mathematics of it at all, there is so much, and people think these Tour players make it easy. Well, it's not. I love hearing the people whisper

People think that golf is all about the glamor and it's easy to do since the public hears what they get paid and all the perks, but it's not. No matter what, outsiders don't have a clue. When your husband hits a ball into the trees, it's painful.

in the gallery about my husband or expressing their general interest in Jay Don the golfer. Once a woman asked Jay Don to autograph her derriere, and he did just that, walking off the 18th green. Later she realized that I was his wife, but it never bothered me one bit. After all, it's the excitement of golf, and, hopefully, the pleasure that people get from your husband doing his job.

— *Marci Blake*

Simply handling the ups and downs, wins and losses of weekly competition can be difficult. I always try to remember that there is always next week. When you have 40 to 45 events each year to play in, I tell Harrison that there are 40 more to play. The good weeks on tour often come when you least expect it. For example, sometimes after you miss three to four cuts in a row. The losses can be hard to handle and the hurt is felt by both of us. I have often wanted to cry for Harrison because I can see the disappointment in his eyes even though he is putting up a brave front. The first time he got close to winning and came in second place was the easiest to shake off. He was a rookie on tour and this was a new experience—we were just so proud that he held on to the end of the tournament. Over the past three years, Harrison has encountered other close losses and several seconds and thirds. Now he expects so much of himself and those are more difficult to shake off. We usually try not to worry about cuts—you make some and you miss some. That's just the game of golf. How we face adversity is to remember that for every bad day, there will be good days when every putt will fall. Most importantly, focus on the future, not the past.

How we face adversity is to remember that for every bad day, there will be good days when every putt will fall. Most importantly, focus on the future, not the past.

— *Allison Frazar*

Have I Got a Story for You

*Whether it's humorous or provocative,
these anecdotes provide a rare glimpse and
insight into life, which is all but mundane.*

In 1999 Cam played in a Buy.com event in Monterrey, Mexico. I like to walk ahead of the group, so when the guys were waiting to tee off on the 18th hole, I started walking down the fairway. About halfway down, I spotted a female deer up ahead just off the cart path. She seemed tame, and didn't seem to be bothered by my approach. As I got closer, I stopped and was surprised that she started coming toward me! I

stood still and she walked right up to me—I was speaking softly to her and then started to pet her for just a second. Then the deer turned away from me and started to walk away. I reached out to pet her again and she turned around, reared up, and started batting her paws at me. I jumped back so fast and screamed out—it scared me to death and luckily she didn't get me! Anyway, at this point, the guys had already teed off and were seeing all this—they were laughing their butts off at me. I wish we had caught that on tape! So much for a deer attack! But it didn't end there; on that same hole up by the green, a wasp flew up the back of my shirt and stung me. So there I was, attacked by a deer and stung by a bee in one day on the same hole!

— *Jennifer Beckman*

I'll never forget the time the nurse called to give Fuzzy instructions to go to the hospital for an epidural on his back and she told him to bring a driver. Fuzzy was so perplexed by what the nurse had told him, and asked, "Okay, so which do you prefer, a Mizuno, a Titleist, or a Taylor Made?" I thought to myself, "Oh boy, there's Fuzzy at it again." And quickly explained that she meant a designated driver. After all, he was going to be a little sore. I told Fuzzy, if he felt as if he needed a security blanket, go ahead and take one. That's just Fuzzy; if he can put a smile on someone's face, then he is truly complete. He's that way at home and out on the golf course.

— *Diane Zoeller*

Coming back from Hawaii in 2000, which was our first Tour tournament, and arriving at the next Tour stop at the Hope Classic in Palm Desert was quite an eye-opener. There we were, my wife Nancy, the two children, my caddie Andy, and a million bags of luggage. What did we know about traveling on tour? Not very much! While I knew the Tour provided courtesy cars for the players for free, I had considered renting a van since there were so many bodies and so much luggage. But I figured the car was free and with determination we'd make it all fit into this nice Chrysler sedan that met us curbside at the airport.

As we were standing there, Davis Love walked by us with two small bags and he was eyeing our situation. He turned to me and said, "You will never fit all that crap in there." And walked away.

I thought to myself, "Do we even belong here?" What a very subtle comment and acknowledgement from a fellow player. But that's just Davis's way—a funny little sarcastic quip to let me know he knew who I was and that I knew he was there. We were so determined to make it all fit—everything and everyone—and we did!!

— *Bob Heintz*

Half of the guys on tour couldn't care less that you go out and shoot 80, but I will tell you that the other half wishes that you shot 81.

Haven't you ever noticed that the media just waits to grab onto something, anything, just for print? Well, let me tell you something that was once said to me. I came back from a tournament and marched myself into the locker room all bent out of shape after my round. One of the players turned to me with this smirk on his face and said, "Matt, give me a moment to let you in on a little secret. Half of the guys on tour couldn't care less that you go out and shoot 80, but I will tell you that the other half wishes that you shot 81." How's that for putting things into perspective?

— *Matt Gogel*

In 1977, we had to take a private plane. Billy and I were flying with two other golfing couples. There was a thunderstorm, and the flight was very choppy. One pro and his wife had brought their dog, and the other pro and his wife had brought their cat. One of the golfers had the flu and started throwing up. The cat was also getting sick and spouting from both ends. It was a terrible experience. After the flight, I turned to my husband and said, "Billy Casper, we have ten kids, and I refuse to fly in a private plane again!"

After the flight, I turned to my husband and said, "Billy Casper, we have ten kids, and I refuse to fly in a private plane again!"

— *Shirley Casper*

When I was at the Masters in 1962, young Jack was just a few months old. I was sitting on the porch kind of bemoaning the fact that I missed our baby who was back home. There was an older woman sitting there knitting and not paying too much attention to me in the corner rocking chair. Then all of a sudden she looked up at me and pointed her finger right in my face. "Listen little girl, you had your husband Jack long before you had that baby, and you will hope to have Jack long after that baby is grown up and gone away. Now you had better grow up and be a wife." I was so taken back. After the years went by, and Jack would call me from a tournament and be lonely and ask me to come, I would think how much easier it would be to stay at home with the babies in diapers. And then I would remember that woman and in ten seconds flat, I would say to Jack over the phone that I will be there, and off I went. Actually that woman was Aleta Mangrum, the wife of Lloyd Mangrum who won the Masters in 1946. I didn't see her for about ten years and then we bumped into each other, and I told her that although she might not remember me, I wanted her to know what a profound impact she had on me and my marriage. I tell the young Tour wives the same story today. You have got to be out there, and you have got to be there with your husband—

and it is you who must make sacrifices to be part of his life. I only hope they will pass this bit of advice along to others. It

used to amaze me that in a crowd of 30 or 40 thousand people my husband would say to me after the tournament, "So where were you on the eighth hole?" I didn't even have a clue that Jack noticed me out there, and if I actually just stopped to say hello to another Tour wife, sure enough Jack would know when I was there and when I was not. That's how important the "we" is in our lives.

— *Barbara Nicklaus*

You have got to be out there, and you have got to be there with your husband— and it is you who must make sacrifices to be part of his life.

I used to play Australian-rules football where there were 18 players on a team. As a sport the other 17 could make you look good, or make you look bad. I got to the point where I was probably the best player on our team, and when the age groups got bigger and more physical, all they wanted to do was try and beat me up every week. I got sick of that. I played golf with a friend. I managed to do pretty good out on the course without formal lessons or anything, and after a while I was getting pretty good at the game. I really enjoyed it, just practicing and trying different shots. I found out it was a fun game, and I liked the different elements, all the wind. I like the wind. Playing in the wind is not all that difficult since I grew up that way. I've had some of my best scores in the wind because it makes me concentrate more or think more. I've shot my course records in horrible conditions. Perfect days get me!

— *Bradley Hughes*

While other sports have mascots, I believe that I could be a poster child for Qualifying School. After all, I've almost lost count on how many times I've tried to get my Tour card back. I could have set an all-time record! It sure seems that way. With some equipment changes in the past years, I lost the fundamentals of my game, and I got really, really screwed up to put it mildly. At that time, I felt as though my whole world collapsed. I lost control of my swing and self-worth as a golfer. I had to do something since I needed to make a living, and I wasn't cutting it at playing golf.

My goal is to keep my card so I can gracefully make the transition to the Senior Tour as I get older. Those guys seem to be having some fun.

I started a business selling synthetic greens. There I was trying to sell something and I'm not a businessman. I knew nothing more about what it took to be a salesperson than the man in the moon. As a matter of fact, I was so apologetic to the customers, I spent more time talking them out of the product instead of selling it. So there I was even bad at that. But I did build one in the backyard of my house and I would go back there (sneaking) with my wedge in one hand and a bucket of balls hitting those wedge shots on the fake greens. I would wonder what would become of me. And the longer I stayed there hitting the wedge shots, the stronger and stronger my game got. I noticed that my confidence started to come back. With the support and determination of my family and my cousins, I was able to see myself get back on tour, and I did just that after a very low period. My goal is to keep my card so I can gracefully make the transition to the Senior Tour as I get older. Those guys seem to be having some fun. And if I can do that, then I can reap the benefits of our pension, retirement and some of the other perks that come along with this job. In a few years, I look forward to a few gray hairs and some change left over in my pocket.

— *David Peoples*

When you are out there playing it's a whole different situation. My friend once gave me some advice and I didn't do it. He told me you should go out to every golf tournament on a Monday, find out the hotels where the best Tour players are staying and call them and let them know that you have a thousand dollars in your pocket. Make sure you make arrangements to go out and play them on Tuesday before the tournament, and while you could potentially lose over $30,000 a year doing this, the experience you get playing with these guys will be invaluable to you. You will never be intimidated when you are paired with them on the tee. I wish I had followed that advice. That's what I would say to all the young guys out there trying a go at this job.

— Tom Jenkins

I have a bad habit of biting my fingernails, so on occasion, I wear those dime store fake ones. Well, at one tournament I saw Bob limping down the fairway. He stopped on the course, took off his shoes and tried to see what was there. Since he couldn't find any-thing, he be-gan to take his socks off as well. In  one of his socks was my red fingernail. He took it out, looked for me, walked over, and said, "I think you lost something."

— Shari Duval

When Doug was leading the rain-delayed 2000 Senior PGA Championship at PGA National in West Palm Beach, Florida, we tested our system. Our daughter-in-law, Sonia, was due to deliver our third grandchild (Jay and Sonia's first child) in two weeks. Tuesday, the day before I left to join Doug, I stood in the kitchen and said, "You know what my worst nightmare would be? Sonia will go into labor, and Dad will be leading the tournament." I really had no premonition about Doug winning that week, but I just knew that sometimes in life we are presented with difficult choices, and that would certainly be one!

> *Being a Tour wife often put me in the position of making choices, but none so gut-wrenching as this.*

We were staying with our daughter Kristi and her husband Pat in Boca Raton. Doug was leading, and Sunday morning at 7:50 A.M., the phone rang. Jay and Sonia were on their way to the hospital. I was overcome with emotion. I really did have to make a choice. Tears come to my eyes even now as I relive that moment. How could I leave Doug at a time that could be one of the most important of his 25-year career…the possibility of him winning not only his first Senior PGA Tournament, but also his first major championship? Yet, how could I not be there to see Jay's first child come into this world and into our family?!

Being a Tour wife often put me in the position of making choices, but none so gut-wrenching as this. Finally, as Doug and I held each other and thanked God for this special time, we both cried. They were tears of joy and hopeful expectation. The decision was this: Doug had Kristi and Pat to share whatever happened there. I should go be with Sonia and Jay. I quickly changed my airline reservation and arrived at the hospital 20 minutes after Carson Isaac Tewell was born. What a joyous moment!

— *Pam Tewell*

One of the first years I was on tour with George, I hadn't done much traveling. It was March 1966 and we were driving from California to Florida. We pulled into a small town in Texas. I have no sense of direction or space. George was really tired so he and our girls went to the room. He asked me to please go get hamburgers because he was starving. I got the hamburgers and then I got lost. I drove around for three hours having no idea where I was. Finally, I recognized our motel. When I walked into the room George and the babies were sound asleep. George then asked, "Why are the hamburgers so cold?"

...If there are "golf groupies," I'm oblivious to them. I don't pay any attention to them. However, there was this one girl that followed George. She would talk to his caddie. One day, she positioned herself so everyone could see her. She was standing near me. As George approached me, she tried to get closer, and slid— all the way down the hill in the mud. We never saw her again.

— *Donna Archer*

So what about Tom Kite having a collision with a bird? That's happened to me, but not in a tournament. I hit a bird out on the golf course one day with my ball. The bird pitched itself up in the cup together with my ball and I made a birdie. Two birdies for me in one hole was really something.

— *Jack Nicklaus*

The bird pitched itself up in the cup together with my ball and I made a birdie. Two birdies for me in one hole was really something.

Jay Don had been asking me out for almost four years and I wouldn't go out with him because I was a single mom, and because I wouldn't date a customer! I had worked at a leather store in Las Vegas and he came in to buy a jacket for his girlfriend at the time. I sold him the jacket, and he kept calling and asking me out. He told me at the time he was going to marry me but I didn't pay attention to that since guys would always come in there and ask me out, and also because it was Las Vegas!

Jay Don and I had our first official date at the Masters in 1993. He rented this beautiful house in Augusta for the tournament and his brother Ward was there with us. I felt like Cinderella. I had this incredible princess suite downstairs with a canopied bed and a mixture of old antiques in the sitting area filled with wicker furniture. During the week of the tournament, he went to the mall and bought this big cookie that said, "Marci will you marry me?" I was a little in shock. It was our first date, and he wanted to marry me? The next day we are out on the course and I told him that if he won this tournament, I would marry him. I didn't have a clue what this golf was all about or what he was doing out there! He gave me a look like, "You don't even know what is going on here!" I told my Dad what happened and he said I wasn't cool at all.

It took us about five years to get married. After all, golfing took him all over the place, and I had responsibilities of my own. I finally accepted a ring from my knight in shining armor in the back of his house on the putting green. Then, he again proposed to me in a sky lit with fireworks in front of all our children at Busch Gardens during the Williamsburg tournament in 1994. I always worked really hard, and never got to see the sunsets, smell the roses or even experience the outdoors and all the places we now go to together as a family. I am truly grateful.

— *Marci Blake*

The Tour today doesn't build interpersonal relationships. When we were on Tour a long time ago, we were all on top of each other and knew just about everything about another player, their family and what was going on in their lives. That just doesn't exist today. It's not a user-friendly locker room. When I was on tour, I can remember when a player walked in the locker room, and the other golfers would turn around and say, "Hello Mr. Irwin." Or, "Hello, Mr. Nicklaus." Or, "Hi, Mr. Barber." Today you walk into that same locker room and you hardly even get an acknowledgement, and believe me, they know who you are.

A prime example happened a while back at Pinehurst during the 1999 U. S. Open when Jack Nicklaus shot 78. I walked into the players' dining area where there were all these huge tables for the players and their families. Every table was filled, and there was Jack sitting all alone. I grabbed a sandwich and asked him if he minded if I joined him, and he said, "Hey, Jerry—pull up a chair, after all I am alone." That would never have happened years ago. We've lost that special part of interest in each other as golfers and as human beings. Today the stakes are higher and the goals are tougher, but the fact remains we have lost that sense of camaraderie of knowing and wanting to know each other outside of our jobs.

— *Jerry Pate*

We've lost that special part of interest in each other as golfers and as human beings. Today the stakes are higher and the goals are tougher, but the fact remains we have lost that sense of camaraderie of knowing and wanting to know each other outside of our jobs.

I remember when we had our first little girl and she was probably a month or two. We were in Florida. I was strolling her along watching Mike, counting my blessings, and thinking, "When she is five, Mike will have been on the Tour for ten years. I'm sure by then we'll have a real job and be home." I don't know if I ever saw myself living my life on tour for a long time. But as I look back, the weeks in a hotel room with my children were the best. I enjoyed mothering so much. Our imaginations made hotel rooms into many a wonderful place. Playing house with my little girls and their toys, "My Little Ponies," "Duplo" Blocks, puzzles, cuddling up and reading stories in bed. Talking when the lights were out. The children seemed to know that if Dad played good that day all were happy; if he didn't, they needed to be on guard, and Dad needed lots of hugs and kisses. Mike realized that there was something outside of golf that brought great joy and peace and that was a family. The family unit is so important, but if not fed and nurtured can be destroyed.

For Mike and me, when our daughter got married we felt as if our greatest masterpiece was almost finished, but now another artist and

the masterpiece decided to finish it, and we put the brushes down and watched it go to another studio for the added finishes. We put our life into the painting and it's hard to watch it leave. But now we need to step back and focus on our other pieces of art and continue with them. In some ways I think Mike feels that golf has robbed him of time with the art created. I see him wanting to leave golf for a time. It can be fulfilling but not when your family grows up and you missed much of it. I know he has some regrets, but when you talk to our children, especially the three oldest, they have none. They know their dad was only a phone call away and that he truly loves them. He loves golf but it is a means to an end not the living end. What more can a child ask for? Mike has his priorities in the right place.

As I look back, the weeks in a hotel room with my children were the best. I enjoyed mothering so much. Our imaginations made hotel rooms into many a wonderful place.

— *Randolyn Reid*

Fred Couples was my guy when I was growing up. I met him in 1992. In fact, it was the week before he won the Masters. We were at River Oaks in Houston, Texas. I was still in college and I was with my golf team. We were able to sit and watch Freddie hit golf balls, and he spoke to us. I had watched him play for a long time before that and I thought our personalities matched a little bit in that I'm relaxed and laid back like he is. I wanted to pattern my golf after somebody like him who is like me, if you know what I mean. He talked about how he tries to play the game in a natural way. He tries to visualize shots, hit them, and not be mechanical. He just told us a lot of stuff that made sense to me and really helped me get to where I am today.

— *Cameron Beckman*

Arnold Palmer and I are the best of friends, and he has made a significant mark upon my life. I am the luckiest man to have met such a wonderful human being, and have admired him since I was a little boy. Now I have grown up, so to speak, and together we have evolved as friends. You want to know what it was like the first time I teed it up with the legend himself? It was 1975 in Dallas, and there I was with Arnold Palmer. I was in such awe of this man. All I wanted to do was just to see him in action on the golf course, and there I was. Arnie did everything that was right in the game of golf, and then there I was punching along. Boy, those fairways were awfully long that day and the course just seemed to go on and on. I was fascinated to see what made him tick, and he was truly a gentleman for putting up with me. I was shaking in every sense of the word. The way Arnie treated those people that were around that day touched my life forever, and gave me a model to follow. He is the true gentleman of life. We have had great ones out there on the PGA, but Arnold Palmer is the best, and we continue to be the best of friends. I still laugh about that day.

The way Arnie treated those people that were around that day touched my life forever, and gave me a model to follow. He is the true gentleman of life.

— *Fuzzy Zoeller*

By far the coolest thing that ever happened to me was at the Canadian Open in 1984. It definitely changed my attitude and perspective about things in life. It can be as simple as one incident in life.

On the 11th hole of the tournament, I was faced with making sure that my tee shot stayed in the fairway, and it was even more important on the second shot to the green since there was a river running in front of it. It was critical on this monster par-4 to have your shots clean—this was one of the toughest holes I have ever seen. So there I am with a good tee shot straight down the fairway and I decide to take an iron and place the second shot on the green. Well, I hit one of the worst shots I have ever had in golf; I chunk it and there lands my orange ball in the river and I am out of play. It was no secret that I had one of the most horrible tempers out there on tour, and it would be a good day for my round if I finished with the same 14 clubs that I started the day with. So there I am cussing and steaming to myself as I drop a new ball, hit it on the green, and proceed to walk across the bridge to finish. As I am walking by just as miserable as I could possibly be, I noticed a man with a little girl who wasn't much more than about four years old. She looked so unhappy; with her hands covering her face and her head bowed. I couldn't help but to notice that she looked as miserable out there as I was. So I stopped and asked my caddie to give me a new orange ball from my bag, and I bent down and said, "If I give you an orange ball, would you give me a smile?" She looked up and took the ball, and exchanged with a big smile on her face. I walked on to finish putting out and moved on to the next hole. About an hour later on the course, I recognized the same man and little girl over on the side of the ropes, and I see her waving at me. I walked over, and she handed me a stick of gum and said, "Here, big guy. Now we're even!" And I had the biggest smile on my face at the time.

As simple as it may seem, I realized at that time that I have to appreciate why the people in the gallery are at a tournament. Not all are there for the golf. They are interested in the show, or maybe they have been forced out there to be dragged around because someone else is interested in the game but they aren't. There are so many reasons, but I came to understand how to regulate my patience level so much better—maybe just by engaging in a simple smile out on the golf course.

— *John Adams*

Traveling as a family with the children out on tour has definitely been the highlight for Larry and me. As the children get older, every year there are new and exciting things to see and do out there. We have made wonderful memories that we'll never forget and we are all so fortunate. Our biggest and most recent memory is climbing down 32 flights of stairs at our hotel in Las Vegas in 1999, when an earthquake awakened us at 3 A.M. Larry and I were with our son Devon (age 11). It was tough to convince Devon that we were in the "emergency mode" and needed to act quickly. But as he noticed the chandelier swinging and things falling, he began to take it seriously. For the next three nights, I kept feeling that the room was swaying, so I kept a glass of water beside my bed and if the water was still, I knew that my imagination was not!!

Even the time we had an unwanted mouse living with us in a hotel room in Williamsburg couldn't dampen our spirits.

Even the time we had an unwanted mouse living with us in a hotel room in Williamsburg couldn't dampen our spirits. My children and husband returned from dinner that evening only to find that the room they left was vacant and I had moved us all to another place. These situations are the ones that you most remember and get a kick out of.

— *Jan Rinker*

There I was at the U.S. Open in Shinnecock, New York, having dinner with my wife Crystol and Neil Lancaster. It was a Friday and I had just missed the cut, and was practicing on some swing flaws at the driving range. Neil turned to me and said, "Man, I barely remembered to register for the Hartford Open next week." I immediately thought to myself, "Oh shit, I did forget to register for the Hartford Open next week." Now, here I am having to tell my wife I messed up. We're only an hour or so from the next tournament site, already on the East Coast, and I've really screwed this one up. Now we have nowhere to go. Damn, was Crystol mad at me! She was pissed and with good reason. Registering for a tournament seems like such an easy thing, all you have to do is make a call the week before by 5 P.M. and it's all taken care of. But it's not! I'd bet that almost every pro on tour has done that same thing because, if you think you are in every tournament, the days out there on tour just slide. I get so caught up in taking care of what I have to do, it's a tough deal sometimes. I've learned my lesson well, and now I'll go and commit to every tournament I know I am playing at the beginning of the year and, instead of my remembering to call, the tournament officials now call me to check and make sure I still plan on coming to play. Out in the golf world, there are so many things going on in your life at all times—practicing, playing, traveling, building time blocks that work, and trying to be flexible.

Out in the golf world, there are so many things going on in your life at all times—practicing, playing, traveling, building time blocks that work, and trying to be flexible.

— *Mike Springer*

A unique way we traveled the Tour for two years was in a 37-foot motor home. We towed a Jeep behind the R.V. and made our way across the country. This was an interesting way to travel after 11 years of flying. It was great the way we could bring part of "home" with us. The boys had their bikes and toys and the same bed each night. We experienced many awesome parks and sights like the Grand Canyon while traveling this way. One year when we left Orlando for California, we had all three boys come down with chicken pox. At least we were contained in our own home!

— *Melissa Peoples*

I never idolized any one person or any one golfer when I was younger. You know, I grew up in Texas, and every day I went out to hit balls or play as a youngster, Charles Coody, who at the time was the director of golf at Fairway Oaks in Texas, was at the range or out on the golf course. Our families were pretty close, and I never thought of him as someone to idolize. But, as I look back, I believe Charles

gave me an opportunity to see what is real, what is important in life, and that there is just a regular person inside the label of a professional golfer. He was like a dad, in that he showed caring to all the kids and he wasn't thought of for his golf however good or bad he was. Maybe that rubbed off on me a little.

— *Mike Standly*

Because of rain delays early in the week, we played back-to-back rounds on Sunday to finish the 2001 Bell South Classic. A 36-hole final day isn't so unusual on Tour, but it became a laundry dilemma for me. I hadn't expected such cold weather in the spring in Atlanta, and had only packed one turtleneck. I wore it under a golf shirt during a practice round on Tuesday, which I played with Carl Paulson. Then I had to wear it under a different golf shirt for the Pro-Am on Wednesday. I happened to be paired with Carl again for my Thursday and Friday rounds. I knew I'd better wash that turtleneck, or even buy another one. But with the rain delays, I just never got the chance. After the second round ended on Saturday, I could have done laundry but by this time, I was leading the tournament. There was no way I could wash my lucky shirt now. I went on to win the event and got a phone message afterward from Carl, who had seen me on TV. He said, "Way to go buddy. But I've just got to ask you, how bad does that black turtleneck smell?"

— *Scott McCarron*

In 1998 I am 135th on the money list, and playing the last tournament of the year at Disney where I shoot three under the first day. Friday the second day, I triple bogey the fifth hole and am just reeling. I end up shooting five over on the front nine. I am already two over par with nine holes to play and the cut is going to be even par. The wind is just howling, and I know I have to shoot two under just to make the cut. I hole out a pitching wedge on the 13th from the rough for an eagle and make the cut. I end up on Saturday shooting five under and now find myself in about 30th place. I realize I've got a chance. On the first tee Sunday I am so nervous, I barely get my ball out on the fairway, and it is not a very pretty-looking shot. My wife Jan comes up to me and says, "Larry, you were shaking on that shot." And I acknowledge to her that I did exactly that. She turns to me again and says, "Come on, you can do it." I figure I am in my home territory, and have to give it my all. I end up eagling that hole 177 yards out, and shooting 68 that day. I move to finish 124th on the money list, and that means I will go on and play next year. *Golf World* listed this round as one of the top ten rounds of the year. I am the only guy who isn't in the top 125 that goes into 125. It is one of the gutsiest performances I ever had, and it is a critical time because I am playing for my whole next season and that's huge. That was my Tour school.

— *Larry Rinker*

Maybe if I had been taller, I would have pursued my interest in football since I really enjoyed the team aspect of the game. But I'm not the right size, and size matters! Taking up golf got to a point that it provided a basis of competitiveness that I thrived on. Playing with my friend Gary Nicklaus on the Ohio State golf team was one of my best experiences. We'd laugh in college when Gary's dad Jack would show up at a tournament when we were playing our matches against other colleges. Nobody could play from the other teams once they caught a glimpse of who was watching. They were too concerned about how their swing looked, or what shot they made, as Jack Nicklaus stood there. It was hysterical to see those guys crumble. Playing on the college team provided me with a solid foundation, exposure and great experience. Yes, our team was a little shaky sometimes in the beginning. We looked at Gary as just one of the regular guys on the team, and he's just that. But when you are growing up and remember watching Jack Nicklaus on TV burning up the courses, and then years later you are standing there with him in the wings—that's an adjustment to say the least!

— *Chris Smith*

Sometimes it's all about being able to pick up the slack! When Bob was playing in the 2002 Shell Open in Houston, I went into labor with our third child. He had called me in the early morning hours before his tee time to see how I was and promised to call when he made the turn during his round. Bob did call as he made his way from the ninth hole to the tenth tee to check on my progress in the hospital. I was doing fine but Daniel was born without Bob there. Since he had been playing crappy for a while and was just a little distracted by the events of the day, Bob missed the cut. I am sure the combination was a catalyst and the result was that Bob wouldn't be playing in the tournament on the weekend. That particular Saturday morning was our family ritual at our country club back home. The Easter Bunny brunch was always a highlight we all looked forward to.

Since I was in the hospital with a day-old newborn, and Bob wouldn't be arriving until that Saturday evening, I decided I needed to pull myself together for our other children. I showered in the hospital, got myself together as best I could, left my newborn in the maternity ward and took the children myself to their "special" event. We had lunch with the Easter Bunny and went about our family time.

— Nancy Heintz

Jim Swaggerty was the first golf coach that stood by me and shaped me as a professional. I was a student at Cal Poly majoring in natural resource management (that stands for "no real major") and Jim was the PGA professional at San Luis Obispo Country Club where I worked as a bag boy. Although he would drill me out there hitting balls, Jim taught me something that helped me to create myself as a professional in a job. Jim taught me all the intangibles. He got me my first car to drive to tournaments, taught me how to travel, how to pack, and everything else about what you had to do to actually be employed as a touring professional. This was a special moment in my life, when this gentleman taught me about life in this profession. It would impact me for the rest of my life. While we spent

I am driven by the negativity of the game— the adversity, if you will.

hours and hours on the range together, he would motivate me to get better by saying, "Loren you are burning daylight," and that would mean I needed to get focused mechanically, and then he would call my very best friends and tell them not to spoil me. It was this type of negative motivation, if you please, that drives me in this career of mine. I am definitely more empowered as an individual based on the amount of negative feedback and thoughts that I come across. I am driven by the negativity of the game—the adversity, if you will.

— Loren Roberts

Jim's fight is missing the integral parts of the children's lives. He wants to be involved at any length whatsoever, regardless of what our issues may be, even after one of his own bad days. This fraction in the family unit is difficult, but regardless, we are strong believers in communicating and respecting the family as a whole entity. For the longest time, my oldest son would say to Jim, "When are you going to bring me a trophy home?" And Jim would tell him that he was going to really, really try hard this time. This dialogue went on for years.

I want the children to understand what it is that Jim does, and I want them to understand what goals mean, and what the benefits of hard work are.

When Jim finally won a tournament, he called our boys and said, "Guess what happened today?" And the boys told him they saw it on TV, and it meant that he would bring them the trophy. Well, when Jim walked through the door and held it up, our children just embraced it.

Shane brought it to school the next day, and held it up in school telling all the children, "My dad did this—he won this." I want the children to understand what it is that Jim does, and I want them to understand what goals mean, and what the benefits of hard work are. You just have to give it all you have.

— *Cyndi Carter*

Index of Contributors

Italics indicate family photos